LITERARY YARNS

LITERARY
YARNS

CROCHET PROJECTS INSPIRED
BY CLASSIC BOOKS

by

CINDY WANG

QUIRK BOOKS
PHILADELPHIA

HOOKS AND BOOKS!

OUR STORY BEGINS . . .

I learned to crochet out of boredom. I started out making little plushies called *amigurumi*, and thus my addiction began. I crocheted a little Frida Kahlo, a fuzzy Link from *The Legend of Zelda*, a miniature Walter White from *Breaking Bad*, a darling Harley Quinn from the Batman series, and on and on. Then my crafting took a literary turn, and the results—the cuddly bookish action figures you've always wanted—are in the pages that follow. With these patterns, you'll impress your literary-minded friends by making everyone's favorite characters.

So go forth, and be the best hooker you can be!

PLOTTING IT OUT

If you've never picked up a crochet hook, learn the basics before tackling these patterns. My favorite resource is PlanetJune.com by June Gilbank, who offers well-written easy-to-follow tutorials.

Every Stitch in the Book

The patterns use abbreviations to indicate stitches and directions. **[Square brackets]** enclose a group of stitches you'll repeat. **(Parentheses)** within brackets further set off a group of stitches. **{Curly brackets}** show the total stitches you should end up with in that line.

ABBREVIATIONS			
ch	chain	sc	single crochet
dc	double crochet	sl st(es)	slip stitch(es)
dec	decrease	st(s)	stitch(es)
hdc	half double crochet	tr	triple crochet
inc	increase		

On the following pages are the special crochet and sewing techniques you'll need.

Magic Ring

Here's how to start a spiral without leaving a small hole in the center.

1 Make a loop with the yarn, placing the working end over the loose end.

2 Insert a crochet hook into the ring, hook it onto the working end of the yarn, and draw the hook back through the loop.

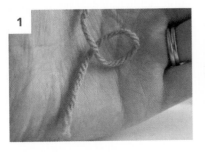 

3 Yarn over the hook and make a chain stitch.

4 Insert the hook back into the loop, making sure to place the hook underneath both yarn tails in the loop. You're going to make your first single crochet stitch in the ring.

5 Yarn over and draw up a loop. There should be 2 loops on the hook.

6 Yarn over and draw up through both loops on the hook. This will complete a single crochet stitch.

7 Repeat as many times as the pattern indicates, taking care to insert the hook under both yarn tails each time you make a new stitch.

8 Hold on to the loose yarn tail and pull to close the loop.

9 To continue in a spiral, crochet back into the first stitch. Make a slip stitch in the first single crochet stitch to finish off with a small ring.

Front Loops vs. Back Loops

Some of the instructions in this book specify "in back loops only." What does that mean? Hold your work upright, with the front facing you. From above it should look like a row of Vs. The row of loops closest to you are the front loops, and the loops farthest from you are the back loops.

FRONT LOOPS

BACK LOOPS

You may also see the instruction "hdc 1, ch 1 and **sl st in the front two loops of the previous hdc.**" When you look at your work from the front, the front two loops of the stitch will be the two loops directly below your hook. Here's how this looks on a double crochet stitch.

Closing Off Pieces

Here's the best way to close off a piece, as brilliantly invented by June Gilbank of PlanetJune.com.

1 When you've reached the last stitch of your piece, cut the yarn, leaving a tail for sewing, and pull the yarn tail through. Identify the front and back loops in the center circle of stitches.

2 Working in the same direction that you crocheted in, thread the yarn tail onto a tapestry needle and insert it in only the front loop of the first stitch, going from the center out. Pull the yarn taut.

3 Repeat around the circle: Insert the needle in only the front loop of the next stitch, going from the center out. Continue doing so until you have threaded the yarn tail through all the stitches around the circle.

4 Grasp the yarn tail and pull tightly. The ring will close. Thread the yarn tail back onto the tapestry needle. Insert the needle into the center of the closed ring.

5 Pull the needle out the other side of the piece. Cut the yarn tail close to the surface of the fabric, give the piece a squeeze, and the yarn tail will be sucked back inside.

Joining Pieces

Open pieces can be sewn together using a simple whipstitch.

1 Line up the open ends of two pieces, with one of the yarn tails inside and the other, which should be long, left outside for sewing.

2 Thread a tapestry needle with the yarn tail. Bring the needle through one of the stitches on the opposite piece, from the outside of the piece in (as shown in the photo; you can work from the inside out, too, as long as you're consistent throughout the edges of the pieces you're joining).

3 Bring the yarn through the edge of the first piece, from the inside out, and pull it through.

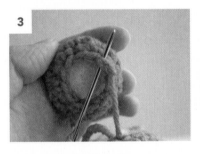

4 Continue stitching around the pieces, each time inserting the needle in the stitch adjacent to the previous one.

5 When you reach the end, fasten off and weave in the end.

Basic Body

This shape is the foundation of several patterns in this book.

Round 1: Sc 5 in magic ring. {5}

Round 2: [Sc 2 in one stitch] 5 times. {10}

Round 3: [Sc 1, sc 2 in next stitch] 5 times. {15}

Round 4: [Sc 2, sc 2 in next stitch] 5 times. {20}

Round 5: [Sc 3, sc 2 in next stitch] 5 times. {25}

Round 6: In back loops only, sc 25. {25}

Rounds 7–11: Sc 25. {25}

Round 12: [Sc 3, dec 1] 5 times. {20}

Round 13: [Sc 2, dec 1] 5 times. {15}

TUTORIALS

LONG HAIR

Make your hairstyle the same color yarn as the rest of the hair. These photos show a contrasting color so the technique is easy to see.

1 Cut several yarn strands twice as long as you want the hair to be. When in doubt, go too long rather than too short; then trim in step 4 if necessary.

2 Insert the crochet hook into one of the front loops of a hairline stitch and hook the midpoint of one of the yarn strands onto the hook. Using a smaller hook may help.

3 Pull the yarn strand through the loop. Wrap the two ends around the hook and pull through. This is called a cow hitch knot.

4 Repeat steps 2–3 around the head. Fill the crown of the head and the sides of the face, but for the remaining parts you may cover only every other row. Trim hair to your liking.

COMBED-BACK HAIR

Used for Jay Gatsby.

1 Thread a tapestry needle with about 24 inches of yarn. Bring the needle through the head at the point where the hairline and the side of the face meet. Knot the inside end.

2 Reinsert the needle at a spot two rows up and on a sharp angle. Bring it back out next to the starting point.

3 Reinsert the needle at the same point above the hairline, forming a narrow inverted V. Bring it back out at a point next to the previous stitch.

4 Reinsert the needle at a point next to the vertex of the previous V-shaped stitch. Bring it back out at a point next to the previous stitch. Reinsert the needle at the same previous point above the hairline, forming a second narrow inverted V.

5 Repeat this process across the hairline. When you reach the opposite side of the face, weave in the tail or tie it to a stitch on the inside of the head.

SIDESWEPT BANGS

Follow the directions for Combed-Back Hair (above), but begin 1 to 2 stitches to the side of the face one row above the hairline and bring the bangs down at a sharp angle onto the forehead. The vertex of the narrow V shape you create should be on the forehead.

SURFACE CHAIN

Used for several characters, including Elizabeth Bennet, Dorothy, the Scarecrow, Daisy Buchanan, and Hester Prynne.

1 Insert the crochet hook into a stitch and bring it out through the other side of the stitch.

2 Yarn over the hook and draw up a loop. Use a tapestry needle to pull the tail through to the inside of the fabric.

3 Yarn over the hook again and draw up a loop into a slip stitch.

4 Reinsert the hook into the next stitch and bring it out on the other side of the same stitch.

5 Yarn over the hook and draw up a loop into a slip stitch.

6 Repeat the previous steps to create a chain of slip stitches.

*"It is a truth universally acknowledged,
that a single man in possession of a good fortune,
must be in want of a lot more yarn."*

ELIZABETH BENNET

JANE AUSTEN'S *PRIDE AND PREJUDICE*, 1813

*Boy meets girl. Boy falls in love with girl and proposes marriage.
Girl declines because boy is a jerk. Boy says, "CHALLENGE ACCEPTED."
Quick-witted and good-natured, Elizabeth Bennet dismisses the perks of
financial gain and refuses to settle for anything less than her match, in
smarts and heart. Though Mr. Darcy makes a horrible first impression,
eventually he wins Lizzie over.*

MATERIALS

- Size E and size B or C crochet hooks
- Worsted-weight yarn in brown, cream, and spring green
- 6-mm black plastic safety eyes
- Fiberfill
- Tapestry needle
- Hair spray, optional
- White embroidery floss
- 1/8"-wide white ribbon
- Hot-glue gun
- Brown thread or fabric glue, optional
- Polypellets, optional

NOTES

Work in continuous rounds unless otherwise specified. Use a size E crochet hook except when size B or C is noted.

Make Lizzie a little Mr. Darcy using the variation of Dr. Jekyll and Mr. Hyde on page 107.

HEAD

Round 1: Starting with brown yarn, sc 5 in magic ring. {5}

Round 2: [Sc 2 in one stitch] 5 times. {10}

Round 3: [Sc 2 in one stitch] 10 times. {20}

Round 4: [Sc 3, sc 2 in next stitch] 5 times. {25}

Round 5: [Sc 4, sc 2 in next stitch] 5 times, changing to cream yarn in the last stitch. {30}

Round 6: Sc 9, sc 2 in next stitch, sc 3, changing to brown yarn. Sc 6, sc 2 in next stitch, sc 9, sc 2 in next stitch, changing to cream yarn. {14 cream + 19 brown = 33}

Rounds 7–9: Sc 14, changing to brown yarn. Sc 19, changing to cream yarn. {14 cream + 19 brown = 33}

Round 10: Sc 9, dec 1, sc 3, changing to brown yarn. Sc 6, dec 1, sc 9, dec 1, changing to cream yarn. {13 cream + 17 brown = 30}

Round 11: [Sc 4, dec 1] twice, sc 1, changing to brown yarn. Sc 3, dec 1, [sc 4, dec 1] twice, changing to cream yarn in the last stitch. {11 cream + 14 brown = 25}

Round 12: [Sc 3, dec 1] twice, sc 1, changing to brown yarn. Sc 2, dec 1, [sc 3, dec 1] twice, changing to cream yarn in the last stitch. {9 cream + 11 brown = 20}

Round 13: [Sc 2, dec 1] twice, sc 1, changing to brown yarn. Sc 1, dec 1, [sc 2, dec 1] twice. {7 cream + 8 brown = 15}

Fasten off and tuck in the end. Attach eyes between rows 8 and 9 (three rows below the hairline), approximately 6 stitches apart. Stuff head firmly with fiberfill.

BUN

Round 1: With brown yarn, sc 5 in magic ring. {5}

Round 2: [Sc 2 in one stitch] 5 times. {10}

Round 3: [Sc 1, sc 2 in next stitch] 5 times. {15}

Round 4: [Sc 2, sc 2 in next stitch] 5 times. {20}

Round 5: Sc 20. {20}

Round 6: [Sc 2, dec 1] 5 times. {15}

Round 7: [Sc 1, dec 1] 5 times. {10}

Fasten off and leave a tail for sewing. Flatten the bun and sew it high on the back of Elizabeth's head.

To make Lizzie's flower: Using white embroidery floss and a B- or C-sized hook, make a magic ring, and [ch 3, sl st into magic ring] 5 times. Pull the center of the magic ring closed.

Cut a 5-inch length of ribbon and wrap it around Elizabeth's hair bun. Either glue in place with a hot-glue gun or tie it off and tuck in the loose ends. Sew or glue the flower to a spot of your choice along the ribbon.

HAIR WISPS AND BANGS

Cut a 2½-inch length of brown yarn and split it in half lengthwise. Thread one of the half-strands through a single stitch at the point where Elizabeth's hair and face intersect (A). Tie the half-strand to the stitch, leaving a length to dangle from the side of her face, and tuck the loose end back into the head (B). Repeat on the other side of her head, and trim as necessary. You may isolate the wisps and spray them with hair spray to prevent fraying and to help them hold their shape.

Cut four 5-inch strands of brown yarn. At the row where Elizabeth's forehead and hairline meet, insert a crochet hook into a stitch immediately to the right of the center of her forehead. A smaller hook may be easier to slide under a stitch. Yarn over the hook with the midpoint of one of the four strands (C), pull up a loop, and then wrap the two loose ends over the hook and pull them into a cow hitch knot (D; see page 11).

Repeat on the stitch immediately to the left of the previous stitch and in the two stitches in the row immediately above it (in her hair; E).

Split the yarn strands lengthwise to make Elizabeth's bangs fuller, then lay them over her forehead and over the hair wisps to create her swept-back bangs. Leave her hair as is or secure the ends of the bangs to the sides of her head, either with small stitches of brown thread or fabric glue (F).

BODY

Work from the bottom up.

Round 1: With spring-green yarn, sc 5 in magic ring. {5}

Round 2: [Sc 2 in one stitch] 5 times. {10}

Round 3: [Sc 1, sc 2 in next stitch] 5 times. {15}

Round 4: [Sc 2, sc 2 in next stitch] 5 times. {20}

Round 5: [Sc 3, sc 2 in next stitch] 5 times. {25}

Round 6: In back loops only, sc 25. {25}

Rounds 7–11: Sc 25. {25}

Round 12: [Sc 3, dec 1] 5 times. {20}

Round 13: [Sc 2, dec 1] twice, changing to cream yarn in the last stitch. Sc 2, dec 1, sc 2, changing to spring-green yarn. Dec 1, sc 2, dec 1. {6 spring green + 5 cream + 4 spring-green = 15}

Fasten off, leaving a spring-green yarn tail for sewing.

Hold the body upside down and look for the "skip" on the row of stitches in the back loops. This will be the back of Elizabeth's body. Using spring-green yarn, start 5 rows from the skip and create a surface chain around the body. {25} (See page 13 for more on surface chains.)

Then continue to use the spring-green yarn to crochet the following along the surface chain:

Rounds 1–3: Sc 25. {25}

Round 4: [Sc 3, sc 2 in next stitch] 5 times. {30}

Rounds 5–7: Sc 30. {30}

Round 8: [(Sc, hdc, sc) in next stitch, sl st in next stitch] 15 times.

Stuff the body firmly with fiberfill, or fill with polypellets first and then top off with fiberfill. Align the cream parts of the body piece with Elizabeth's face on the head piece. (This will become the neckline of Elizabeth's dress.) Sew onto the head using a whipstitch. If you'd like to keep the color consistent on the neckline, sew the head and body together using the spring-green yarn tail from the body, switch to a strand of cream yarn when you reach the neckline of the dress, and then resume sewing with the remainder of the spring-green yarn tail.

DRESS DETAILS

With spring-green yarn, ch 8. Fasten off, leaving a tail for sewing. Sew the chain along the neckline of Elizabeth's dress, sewing onto only one side of the chain's loops.

Cut a 12-inch length of ribbon and use a small amount of hot glue to attach the midpoint to the center of Elizabeth's body, where her skirt starts. Secure at a few more points along the sides, and tie the loose ends in a bow in the back. Trim excess.

"'The road to the City of Emeralds is hooked with yellow yarn,' said the Witch, 'so you cannot miss it.'"

DOROTHY, COWARDLY LION, SCARECROW, AND TIN WOODMAN

L. FRANK BAUM'S *THE WONDERFUL WIZARD OF OZ*, 1900

MGM Studios wanted to show off its new Technicolor abilities with Dorothy's ruby-red shoes in the film adaptation of The Wonderful Wizard of Oz, *but in his original novel, L. Frank Baum was all about silver.*

MATERIALS

- Size E crochet hook
- 6-mm black plastic safety eyes
- Tapestry needle
- Fiberfill

FOR DOROTHY:

- Size B or C crochet hook (for Toto only)
- Worsted-weight yarn in brown, cream, white, sky blue, silver glitter, and straw
- 1/8"-wide white ribbon
- Charcoal-gray worsted-weight yarn, or charcoal-gray embroidery floss
- Big-eye needle
- Black embroidery floss and embroidery needle

FOR COWARDLY LION:

- Worsted-weight yarn in marigold and rust
- Cream felt
- Black embroidery floss and embroidery needle
- Hot-glue gun

FOR SCARECROW:

- Worsted-weight yarn in barley, black, brown, and olive green
- 2 approximately 14"-lengths of thin brown cord or embroidery floss
- Brown thread, optional

FOR TIN WOODMAN:

- Worsted-weight yarn in metallic silver or gray
- Red felt
- 1 small snap fastener
- Gray sewing thread and sewing needle
- Hot-glue gun

NOTES

Work in continuous rounds unless otherwise specified.

Use a size E crochet hook for all characters except Toto. Use a size B or C crochet hook for Toto.

You need only a small amount of silver-glitter yarn for Dorothy's slippers. If none is available, you can use light-gray yarn and then paint over the finished slippers with silver-glitter fabric paint.

DOROTHY

HEAD

Round 1: Starting with brown yarn, sc 5 in magic ring. {5}

Round 2: [Sc 2 in one stitch] 5 times. {10}

Round 3: [Sc 2 in one stitch] 10 times. {20}

Round 4: [Sc 3, sc 2 in next stitch] 5 times. {25}

Round 5: [Sc 4, sc 2 in next stitch] 5 times, changing to cream yarn in the last stitch. {30}

Round 6: Sc 9, sc 2 in next stitch, sc 3, changing to brown yarn. Sc 6, sc 2 in next stitch, sc 9, sc 2 in next stitch, changing to cream yarn. {14 cream + 19 brown = 33}

Rounds 7–9: Sc 14, changing to brown yarn, sc 19, changing to cream yarn. {14 cream + 19 brown = 33}

Round 10: Sc 9, dec 1, sc 3, changing to brown yarn. Sc 6, dec 1, sc 9, dec 1, changing to cream yarn. {13 cream + 17 brown = 30}

Round 11: [Sc 4, dec 1] twice, sc 1, changing to brown yarn. Sc 3, dec 1, [sc 4, dec 1] twice, changing to cream yarn in the last stitch. {11 cream + 14 brown = 25}

Round 12: [Sc 3, dec 1] twice, sc 1, changing to brown yarn. Sc 2, dec 1, [sc 3, dec 1] twice, changing to cream yarn in the last stitch. {9 cream + 11 brown = 20}

Round 13: [Sc 2, dec 1] twice, sc 1, changing to brown yarn. Sc 1, dec 1, [sc 2, dec 1] twice. {7 cream + 8 brown = 15}

Fasten off and tuck in the end. Attach eyes between rows 8 and 9 (three rows below the hairline), approximately 6 stitches apart.

HAIR

Cut six 9-inch strands of brown yarn. Make two pigtails following the instructions opposite, using 3 strands of yarn for each pigtail. Using white ribbon, tie off the pigtails with bows.

Stuff head firmly with fiberfill.

With brown yarn, make bangs following the instructions on pages 17–18.

TUTORIAL: PIGTAILS

This cute hairstyle in real life is even cuter on your amigurimi!

1 Cut six 9-inch-long strands of yarn (three for each side of the head). Using a tapestry needle, thread one strand through a single stitch on the side of the head, one row below the hairline.

2 Thread a second strand of yarn through the head one stitch over and one row down from the previous strand. Thread a third strand one stitch over and one row up from the previous strand.

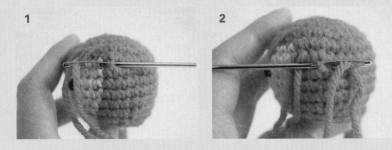

3 Braid the pigtail to your desired length. Tie off braids and trim excess.

BODY

Round 1: Using white yarn, sc 5 in magic ring. {5}

Round 2: [Sc 2 in one stitch] 5 times. {10}

Round 3: [Sc 1, sc 2 in next stitch] 5 times. {15}

Round 4: [Sc 2, sc 2 in next stitch] 5 times. {20}

Rounds 5–8: Sc 20. {20}

Round 9: [Sc 2, dec 1] 5 times. {15}

Fasten off and leave a tail for sewing.

Hold the body upside down and, using sky-blue yarn, create a surface chain between rounds 7 and 8 of the body, two rows from the open end, for a total of 20 stitches. (See page 13 for surface chain instructions.)

Then use sky-blue yarn to crochet along the surface chain:

Round 1: Sc 20. {20}

Round 2: [Sc 3, sc 2 in next stitch] 5 times. {25}

Round 3: Sc 25. {25}

Round 4: [Sc 4, sc 2 in next stitch] 5 times. {30}

Round 5: Sc 30. {30}

Fasten off and weave in the end. Stuff the body firmly with fiberfill and sew it onto the head.

ARMS (MAKE 2)

Round 1: Starting with cream yarn, sc 5 in magic ring. {5}

Round 2: Sc 5, changing to white yarn in the last stitch. {5}

Rounds 3–4: Sc 5. {5}

Fasten off and leave a tail for sewing. Sew onto Dorothy's body.

LEGS (MAKE 2)

Round 1: Starting with silver-glitter yarn, sc 5 in magic ring. {5}

Round 2: Sc 5, changing to cream yarn. {5}

Rounds 3–4: Sc 5. {5}

Fasten off and leave a tail for sewing. Using white yarn, sew a line of backstitches along the color change between silver-glitter and cream yarn to create a sock line. Sew onto Dorothy's body.

DRESS STRAPS (MAKE 2)

Using sky-blue yarn, ch 9 and fasten off, leaving a tail for sewing. Sew onto the body starting from the waistline of Dorothy's dress at the front, continuing over the shoulder, and finishing at the waistline at the back of her dress.

BASKET

Round 1: Using straw yarn, sc 6 in magic ring. {6}

Round 2: [Sc 2 in one stitch] 6 times. {12}

Round 3: In back loops only, sc 12. {12}

Round 4: Sc 12. {12}

Sl st and ch 8 to make the basket handle. Fasten off and leave a short tail for sewing. Sew the end of the chain to the other side of the basket to attach the handle. Weave in the end. Using a short length of straw yarn, sew the center of the basket handle to the end of one of Dorothy's hands, with the open side facing forward so Toto will be visible if placed in the basket. Tuck in the end.

TOTO'S HEAD AND BODY

Round 1: With half-strands of charcoal-gray yarn or strands of charcoal-gray embroidery floss, sc 6 in magic ring. {6}

Round 2: [Sc 2 in one stitch] 6 times. {12}

Round 3: Sc 12. {12}

Stuff the head with a small amount of fiberfill or scrap yarn.

Round 4: Dec 6. {6}

Round 5: In front loops only, [sc 2, sc 2 in next stitch] twice. {8}

Round 6: Sc 8. {8}

Round 7: [Sc 3, sc 2 in next stitch] twice. {10}

Fill with a small amount of fiberfill or scrap yarn.

Round 8: In back loops only, dec 5. {5}

Fasten off and close the piece using a big-eye needle.

TOTO'S SNOUT

Round 1: With half-strands of charcoal-gray yarn or strands of charcoal-gray embroidery floss, sc 4 in magic ring. Sl st. {4}

Fasten off and leave a tail for sewing. Sew onto the head using a big-eye needle. With black embroidery floss and an embroidery needle, embroider a small nose onto the snout using overlapping straight stitches. Sew two French knots on each side of Toto's snout to make his eyes.

EARS (MAKE 2)

With half-strands of charcoal-gray yarn or strands of charcoal-gray embroidery floss, ch 3, then crochet the following:

Row 1: Starting in the 2nd ch from the hook, hdc 1, ch 1. Sl st in the front two loops of the previous hdc. Sl st in the next ch. {1}

Fasten off, leaving a tail for sewing. Gently fold ears in half along the midline and sew onto the head with a big-eye needle. Tuck in the ends.

FRONT LEGS (MAKE 2)

With half-strands of charcoal-gray yarn or strands of charcoal-gray embroidery floss, ch 4, then crochet the following:

Row 1: Starting in the 2nd ch from the hook, sc 3. {3}

Fasten off, leaving a tail for sewing. Sew onto the front of the body directly below the head using a big-eye needle. Tuck in the ends.

HIND LEGS (MAKE 2)

With half-strands of charcoal-gray yarn or strands of charcoal-gray embroidery floss:

Round 1: Sc 3 in magic ring. Sl st to finish off the round. {3}

Fasten off, leaving a tail for sewing. With a big-eye needle, sew legs onto the bottom of the body, offset to the sides to put Toto in a sitting position. Tuck in the ends. Now Dorothy can tote him in her basket!

COWARDLY LION

HEAD

Round 1: With marigold yarn, sc 5 in magic ring. {5}

Round 2: [Sc 2 in one stitch] 5 times. {10}

Round 3: [Sc 2 in one stitch] 10 times. {20}

Round 4: [Sc 3, sc 2 in next stitch] 5 times. {25}

Round 5: [Sc 4, sc 2 in next stitch] 5 times. {30}

Round 6: [Sc 9, sc 2 in next stitch] 3 times. {33}

Rounds 7–9: Sc 33. {33}

Round 10: [Sc 9, dec 1] 3 times. {30}

Round 11: [Sc 4, dec 1] 5 times. {25}

Round 12: [Sc 3, dec 1] 5 times. {20}

Round 13: [Sc 2, dec 1] 5 times. {15}

Fasten off and tuck in the end. Attach eyes between rows 8 and 9, approximately 6 stitches apart. Stuff head firmly with fiberfill. Cut a bean shape out of cream felt to make a snout, and use black embroidery floss and an embroidery needle to embroider a nose on the felt using overlapping straight stitches. Hot-glue the snout onto the face. With rust yarn and a tapestry needle, sew two worried eyebrows over the eyes using overlapping straight stitches.

EARS (MAKE 2)

With marigold yarn, ch 2, then crochet the following:

Row 1: Starting in the 2nd ch from the hook, sc 4 in one stitch. {4}

Fasten off and leave a tail for sewing. Sew onto the head.

MANE

With rust yarn, ch 35. Then crochet the following:

Row 1: Starting in the 2nd ch from the hook, [(sc 1, hdc 1, sc1) in one stitch, sl st] 17 times.

Fasten off, leaving a tail for sewing. Set aside until the head has been sewn to the body.

BODY

Round 1: With marigold yarn, sc 5 in magic ring. {5}

Round 2: [Sc 2 in one stitch] 5 times. {10}

Round 3: [Sc 1, sc 2 in next stitch] 5 times. {15}

Round 4: [Sc 2, sc 2 in next stitch] 5 times. {20}

Rounds 5–8: Sc 20. {20}

Round 9: [Sc 2, dec 1] 5 times. {15}

Fasten off, leaving a tail for sewing. Stuff firmly with fiberfill, then sew onto the head. Sew the mane around the lion's head, taking care to fasten it behind the ears.

ARMS (MAKE 2)

Round 1: With marigold yarn, sc 5 in magic ring. {5}

Rounds 2–4: Sc 5. {5}

Fasten off and leave a tail for sewing.

LEGS (MAKE 2)

Round 1: With marigold yarn, sc 6 in magic ring. {6}

Round 2: Sc 6. {6}

Fasten off and leave a tail for sewing.

Sew the arms and legs to the body, with the legs facing forward and offset to the sides so the lion is sitting. Using a short length of marigold yarn, sew his two front paws together to have him wringing his hands in anxiety.

TAIL

Using marigold yarn, ch 22, then fasten off, leaving a tail for sewing. Weave the other end into the chain.

Using a small amount of rust yarn, tie a cow hitch knot (see page 11) to the woven end of the chain and fray the ends to make the end of the tail. Sew the other end of the tail to his bottom.

SCARECROW

HEAD

Round 1: With barley yarn, sc 5 in magic ring. {5}

Round 2: [Sc 2 in one stitch] 5 times. {10}

Round 3: [Sc 2 in one stitch] 10 times. {20}

Round 4: [Sc 3, sc 2 in next stitch] 5 times. {25}

Round 5: [Sc 4, sc 2 in next stitch] 5 times. {30}

Round 6: [Sc 9, sc 2 in next stitch] 3 times. {33}

Rounds 7–9: Sc 33. {33}

Round 10: [Sc 9, dec 1] 3 times. {30}

Round 11: [Sc 4, dec 1] 5 times. {25}

Round 12: [Sc 3, dec 1] 5 times. {20}

Round 13: [Sc 2, dec 1] 5 times. {15}

Round 14: In front loops only, [sc 1, sc 2 in the next 2 stitches] 5 times. {25}

Round 15: [Sc 3, sc 2 in the next 2 stitches] 5 times. {35}

Fasten off and tuck in the end. Attach eyes between rows 8 and 9, approximately 6 stitches apart. Stuff the head firmly with fiberfill.

HAT

Round 1: With black yarn, sc 3 in magic ring. {3}

Round 2: In back loops only, sc 3. {3}

Round 3: [Sc 2 in one stitch] 3 times. {6}

Round 4: [Sc 1, sc 2 in next stitch] 3 times. {9}

Round 5: Sc 9. {9}

Round 6: [Sc 2, sc 2 in next stitch] 3 times. {12}

Round 7: Sc 12. {12}

Round 8: [Sc 3, sc 2 in next stitch] 3 times. {15}

Round 9: Sc 15. {15}

Round 10: [Sc 4, sc 2 in next stitch] 3 times. {18}

Round 11: Sc 18. {18}

Round 12: [Sc 5, sc 2 in next stitch] 3 times. {21}

Round 13: Sc 21. {21}

Round 14: [Sc 6, sc 2 in next stitch] 3 times. {24}

Round 15: [Sc 7, sc 2 in next stitch] 3 times. {27}

Round 16: [Sc 8, sc 2 in next stitch] 3 times. {30}

Round 17: [Sc 9, sc 2 in next stitch] 3 times. {33}

Round 18: [Sc 10, sc 2 in next stitch] 3 times. {36}

Round 19: In front loops only, [sc 1, sc 2 in the next 3 stitches] 9 times. {63}

Round 20: [Sc 4, sc 2 in the next 3 stitches] 9 times. {90}

Fasten off and weave in the end. Using a length of black yarn and a tapestry needle, sew the hat onto the head. Fold down the tip of the hat.

BODY

Round 1: Starting with brown yarn, sc 5 in magic ring. {5}

Round 2: [Sc 2 in one stitch] 5 times. {10}

Round 3: [Sc 1, sc 2 in next stitch] 5 times. {15}

Round 4: [Sc 2, sc 2 in next stitch] 5 times. {20}

Round 5: Sc 20, changing to olive-green yarn. {20}

Rounds 6–8: Sc 20. {20}

Round 9: [Sc 2, dec 1] 5 times. {15}

Fasten off, leaving a tail for sewing. Stuff body firmly with fiberfill and sew it to the head using a whipstitch, aligning the stitches with the back loops from round 14 of the head. Thread a 14-inch length of brown cord or embroidery floss around the scarecrow's neck and tie it in a bow. Trim excess (A).

SHIRT HEM

Hold the body upside down and, using olive-green yarn, create a surface chain starting at the point where the color change between the brown and olive-green yarn begins. {20} (See page 13 for more on surface chains.) Then continue to use the olive-green yarn to crochet the following along the surface chain:

Round 1: Sc 20. {20}

Fasten off and weave in the end.

Fold a 14-inch length of brown cord or embroidery floss in half and wrap it around his waist. Pull one of the loose ends through the loop and tie the ends in a simple knot (B). Trim excess. Optional: Secure the belt to the waist with a few stitches of brown thread.

ARMS (MAKE 2)

Round 1: Starting with barley yarn, sc 6 in magic ring. {6}

Round 2: Sc 6, changing to olive-green yarn. {6}

Rounds 3–4: Sc 6. {6}

Fasten off, leaving a tail for sewing. Sew arms onto body.

LEGS (MAKE 2)

Round 1: Starting with black yarn, sc 6 in magic ring. {6}

Round 2: Sc 6, changing to brown yarn. {6}

Rounds 3–4: Sc 6. {6}

Fasten off, leaving a tail for sewing. Sew legs onto body.

TIN WOODMAN

HEAD

Round 1: With silver yarn, sc 5 in magic ring. {5}

Round 2: [Sc 2 in one stitch] 5 times. {10}

Round 3: [Sc 1, sc 2 in next stitch] 5 times. {15}

Round 4: [Sc 2, sc 2 in next stitch] 5 times. {20}

Round 5: [Sc 3, sc 2 in next stitch] 5 times. {25}

Round 6: [Sc 4, sc 2 in next stitch] 5 times. {30}

Round 7: In back loops only, sc 30. {30}

Rounds 8–13: Sc 30. {30}

Round 14: In back loops only, sc 30. {30}

Round 15: [Sc 4, dec 1] 5 times. {25}

Round 16: [Sc 3, dec 1] 5 times. {20}

Round 17: [Sc 2, dec 1] 5 times. {15}

Fasten off and weave in the end. Attach eyes between rows 9 and 10, approximately 6 stitches apart. Set aside; do not stuff head until the funnel hat has been sewn on.

FUNNEL HAT

Round 1: With silver yarn, sc 6 in magic ring. {6}

Round 2: In back loops only, sc 6. {6}

Round 3: Sc 6. {6}

Round 4: In front loops only, [sc 2 in one stitch] 6 times. {12}

Round 5: [Sc 3, sc 2 in next stitch] 3 times. {15}

Round 6: [Sc 4, sc 2 in next stitch] 3 times. {18}

Round 7: [Sc 5, sc 2 in next stitch] 3 times. {21}

Round 8: [Sc 6, sc 2 in next stitch] 3 times. {24}

Round 9: [Sc 7, sc 2 in next stitch] 3 times. {27}

Round 10: [Sc 8, sc 2 in next stitch] 3 times. {30}

Round 11: [Sc 9, sc 2 in next stitch] 3 times. {33}

Sl st and ch 8. Fasten off, leaving a short tail for sewing. Sew the end of the chain onto the cone of the funnel to create a small handle.

Using silver yarn, sew the funnel hat onto the head, sewing along round 10 of the funnel and in the back loops of round 7 of the head. This will give the funnel hat a lip. While you sew it on, lightly stuff the hat with fiberfill to hold its shape. Stuff head with fiberfill, again taking care not to stuff too firmly so that it retains its cylindrical shape.

BODY

Round 1: With silver yarn, sc 5 in magic ring. {5}

Round 2: [Sc 2 in one stitch] 5 times. {10}

Round 3: [Sc 1, sc 2 in next stitch] 5 times. {15}

Round 4: [Sc 2, sc 2 in next stitch] 5 times. {20}

Round 5: [Sc 3, sc 2 in next stitch] 5 times. {25}

Round 6: In back loops only, sc 25. {25}

Rounds 7–12: Sc 25. {25}

Round 13: In back loops only, sc 25. {25}

Round 14: [Sc 3, dec 1] 5 times. {20}

Round 15: [Sc 2, dec 1] 5 times. {15}

Fasten off, leaving a tail for sewing. Stuff body with fiberfill, taking care not to overstuff so that it retains its cylindrical shape. Sew onto the head using a whipstitch.

ARMS AND LEGS (MAKE 4)

Round 1: With silver yarn, sc 6 in magic ring. {6}

Round 2: In back loops only, sc 6. {6}

Rounds 3–5: Sc 6. {6}

Fasten off, leaving a tail for sewing. Sew arms and legs onto body.

CHEST PLATE

Using silver yarn, ch 6, then crochet the following:

Row 1: Starting in the 2nd ch from the hook, sc 5, then ch 1 and turn. {5}

Rows 2–4: Sc 5 across, ch 1, and turn. {5}

Fasten off, leaving a tail for sewing. Weave in the starting end. Position the chest plate on the front of the body and sew it to the body on one side to make a flap. Weave in the end. Position a small snap on the opposite side of the "hinge" of the chest plate. With sewing needle and thread, sew one part of the snap to the inside of the chest plate and the other piece to the body opposite the first piece. Cut a small red heart out of felt and carefully hot-glue it to the chest, where it will be covered by the chest plate when the plate is closed.

Optional: For extra charm, embroider an outline of straight stitches along the edge of the heart with embroidery floss.

*"The White Rabbit put on his spectacles.
'Where shall I begin, please your Majesty?' he asked.
'Begin at the beginning,' the King said gravely, 'and single
crochet till you come to the end: then fasten off.'"*

WHITE RABBIT

LEWIS CARROLL'S *ALICE'S ADVENTURES IN WONDERLAND*, 1865

*Punctuality may not be the White Rabbit's strong suit, but he
certainly is dedicated to his appointments and is a loyal servant to the
Queen of Hearts. (Though who wouldn't give 110 percent for a boss who
constantly threatens decapitation?)*

MATERIALS

- Size E crochet hook
- Worsted-weight yarn in white, taupe, and red
- 9-mm black plastic safety eyes
- Tapestry needle
- Pink embroidery floss and embroidery needle, or pink worsted-weight yarn
- Fiberfill
- Polypellets, optional
- 1" square of white felt
- White thread and sewing needle
- Bead or button of your choice, for brooch
- Clock/watch charm (found in the jewelry-making section of craft stores)
- Straight pins with yellow ball pinheads
- Hot-glue gun
- Small white pom-pom

NOTES

Work in continuous rounds unless otherwise specified.

Use yellow embroidery floss and an embroidery needle to sew two French knots onto the jacket if you don't want to use straight pins.

HEAD

Round 1: With white yarn, sc 6 in magic ring. {6}

Round 2: [Sc 2 in one stitch] 6 times. {12}

Round 3: [Sc 1, sc 2 in next stitch] 6 times. {18}

Round 4: [Sc 2, sc 2 in next stitch] 6 times. {24}

Round 5: [Sc 3, sc 2 in next stitch] 6 times. {30}

Round 6: [Sc 4, sc 2 in next stitch] 6 times. {36}

Rounds 7–11: Sc 36. {36}

Round 12: [Sc 4, dec 1] 6 times. {30}

Round 13: [Sc 3, dec 1] 6 times. {24}

Round 14: [Sc 2, dec 1] 6 times. {18}

Fasten off and tuck in the end. Attach eyes between rounds 8 and 9, approximately 6 stitches apart. With pink yarn or embroidery floss and a tapestry needle, sew a series of overlapping straight stitches to create a nose. Stuff head firmly with fiberfill.

EARS (MAKE 2)

Round 1: With white yarn, sc 6 in magic ring. {6}

Round 2: [Sc 2 in one stitch] 6 times. {12}

Rounds 3–8: Sc 12. {12}

Fasten off, leaving a tail for sewing. Flatten ear, sew shut using a whipstitch, and sew to head.

BODY

Round 1: Starting with white yarn, sc 6 in magic ring. {6}

Round 2: [Sc 2 in one stitch] 6 times. {12}

Round 3: [Sc 1, sc 2 in next stitch] 6 times. {18}

Round 4: [Sc 2, sc 2 in next stitch] 6 times. {24}

Round 5: [Sc 3, sc 2 in next stitch] 6 times. {30}

Rounds 6–8: Sc 30, changing to taupe yarn in the last stitch of round 8. {30}

Rounds 9–12: Sc 30. {30}

Round 13: [Sc 3, dec 1] 6 times. {24}

Round 14: [Sc 2, dec 1] 6 times. {18}

Fasten off, leaving a tail for sewing. Stuff the body with fiberfill or with poly-pellets topped with fiberfill. With a tapestry needle whipstitch to the head.

JACKET

Do not count slip stitches in stitch count. Use stitch markers to mark first and last sc of each row. (See page 43.) Using red yarn, ch 37, then crochet:

Row 1: Starting in the 2nd ch from the hook, sc 36 across. Ch 1 and turn. {36}

Row 2: Sc 36, ch 1, and turn. {36}

Row 3: Skip the first sc, then sc 34, sl st in last stitch, ch 1, and turn. {34}

Row 4: Skip the first sc, then sc 32, sl st in last stitch, ch 1, and turn. {32}

Row 5: Skip the first sc, then sc 30, sl st in last stitch, ch 1, and turn. {30}

Row 6: Skip the first sc, then sc 28, sl st in last stitch, ch 1, and turn. {28}

Row 7: Skip the first sc, then sc 26, sl st in last stitch, ch 1, and turn. {26}

Row 8: Skip the first sc, then sc 24, sl st in last stitch. {24}

Fasten off, leaving a tail for sewing.

HIND LEGS (MAKE 2)

Round 1: With white yarn, sc 6 in magic ring. {6}

Round 2: [Sc 2 in one stitch] 6 times. {12}

Round 3: Sc 12. {12}

Fasten off, leaving a tail for sewing.

FRONT PAWS (MAKE 2)

Round 1: With white yarn, sc 6 in magic ring. {6}

Round 2: [Sc 1, sc 2 in next stitch] 3 times, changing to red yarn in the last stitch. {9}

Rounds 3–4: Sc 9. {9}

Fasten off, leaving a tail for sewing.

FINISHING TOUCHES

Bunch up felt on one side to create ruffles for a cravat and sew it together with white thread and a sewing needle. Then sew the bunched end to the body directly under his chin. Sew a button or bead onto the cravat as a brooch.

Fold the top row of the jacket to create a collar/lapel and position the jacket over the body. Pin the jacket in place and sew it to the body with red yarn and a tapestry needle, overlapping the cravat. Sew the jacket closed.

Sew on the paws. Stuff the legs with fiberfill and sew them on, slightly offset so he sits. Sew the clock charm onto a paw. Stick two straight pins into the jacket as buttons. Finally, hot-glue on his small pom-pom tail.

"It has long been an axiom of mine that the little stitches are infinitely the most important."

SHERLOCK HOLMES

ARTHUR CONAN DOYLE'S *THE ADVENTURES OF SHERLOCK HOLMES*, 1892

Sherlock Holmes was brilliant almost to a fault, with an eye for detail that helped him crack cases no one else could solve. If we all had a mind like his, we wouldn't be losing our keys all the time.

MATERIALS

- Size E and size G crochet hooks
- Worsted-weight yarn in brown, cream, taupe, black, and white
- 6-mm black plastic safety eyes
- Stitch markers
- Tapestry needle
- Small amount of black lightweight (#3) yarn or embroidery floss
- Fiberfill
- Polypellets, optional

NOTES

Use a size E crochet hook for all parts unless otherwise specified.

Work in continuous rounds unless otherwise specified.

HEAD

Round 1: Starting with brown yarn, sc 5 in magic ring. {5}

Round 2: [Sc 2 in one stitch] 5 times. {10}

Round 3: [Sc 2 in one stitch] 10 times. {20}

Round 4: [Sc 3, sc 2 in next stitch] 5 times. {25}

Round 5: [Sc 4, sc 2 in next stitch] 5 times. {30}

Round 6: [Sc 9, sc 2 in next stitch] 3 times, changing to cream yarn in the last stitch. {33}

Rounds 7–9: Sc 14, changing to brown yarn, sc 19, changing to cream yarn. {14 cream + 19 brown = 33}

Round 10: Sc 9, dec 1, sc 3, changing to brown yarn. Sc 6, dec 1, sc 9, dec 1, changing to cream yarn. {13 cream + 17 brown = 30}

Round 11: [Sc 4, dec 1] twice, sc 1, changing to brown yarn. Sc 3, dec 1, [sc 4, dec 1] twice, changing to cream yarn in the last stitch. {11 cream + 14 brown = 25}

Round 12: [Sc 3, dec 1] twice, sc 1, changing to brown yarn. Sc 2, dec 1, [sc 3, dec 1] twice, changing to cream yarn in the last stitch. {9 cream + 11 brown = 20}

Round 13: [Sc 2, dec 1] twice, sc 1, changing to brown yarn. Sc 1, dec 1, [sc 2, dec 1] twice. {7 cream + 8 brown = 15}

Fasten off and tuck in the end. Attach eyes between rows 8 and 9 (two rows below the hairline), approximately 6 stitches apart. Stuff head firmly with fiberfill.

HAT

Round 1: With taupe yarn, sc 5 in magic ring. {5}

Round 2: [Sc 2 in one stitch] 5 times. {10}

Round 3: [Sc 1, sc 2 in next stitch] 5 times. {15}

Round 4: [Sc 2, sc 2 in next stitch] 5 times. {20}

Round 5: [Sc 3, sc 2 in the next stitch] 5 times. {25}

Round 6: [Sc 4, sc 2 in next stitch] 5 times. {30}

Round 7: Sc 30. {30}

Round 8: [Sc 5, sc 2 in next stitch] 5 times. {35}

The following will start the front brim of the hat. Do not count the slip stitches in your stitch count. Use stitch markers to mark the first and last sc of each row from this point on. (The technique used for both brims of the hat is the same as that for jackets; see page 43.)

Row 9: In the front loops only, sc 15. Then sl st in next stitch, ch 1, and turn. {15}

Row 10: Skip over the first sc, then sc 2, hdc 2, [hdc 2 in one stitch] 5 times, hdc 2, sc 2, sl st in next stitch, ch 1, and turn. {18}

Row 11: Sc in the sl st from the previous row, then sc 18 across, sc in the last sl st in the previous row. {20}

Sl st and fasten off. Weave in the end.

BACK BRIM

Do not count slip stitches in your stitch count. Use stitch markers to mark the first and last sc of each row.

Using taupe yarn, starting 5 stitches away from the end of the front brim, crochet the following into the edge of the hat:

Row 1: In the front loops only sc 10 across, then sl st, ch ,1 and turn. {10}

Row 2: Sc 3, then [hdc 2 in one stitch] 4 times, sc 3. Sl st, ch 1, and turn. {14}

Row 3: Sc 14 across. {14}

Sl st and fasten off. Weave in the end.

EAR FLAPS (MAKE 2)

Using taupe yarn, ch 3, then crochet the following:

Row 1: Starting in the 2nd ch from the hook, sc 2. Ch 1 and turn. {2}

Row 2: Sc 2, ch 1, and turn. {2}

Row 3: Sc 2 in next stitch, sc 1, ch 1, and turn. {3}

Row 4: Sc 3, ch 1, and turn. {3}

Row 5: Sc 2, sc 2 in next stitch, ch 1, and turn. {4}

Row 6: Sc 5 up one edge of the ear flap, then sc 3 in one stitch when you reach the point of the flap. Sc 5 back down the other side.

Fasten off, leaving a tail for sewing.

Sew flaps onto the edge of the hat in the gaps between the front and back brims, and weave in the ends. Bring the two tips of the flaps together at the top of the hat, then thread a short length of black lightweight yarn through them and tie it a bow. Trim excess. Position the hat onto Sherlock's head and sew on with taupe yarn.

BODY

Starting with black yarn, crochet a Basic Body as on page 11, changing to white yarn in the last stitch of Round 8. Fasten off, leaving a tail for sewing. Stuff the body firmly with fiberfill, or fill with polypellets first and then top off with fiberfill. Sew to the head using a whipstitch.

COAT

Do not count slip stitches in your stitch count. Use stitch markers to mark the first and last sc of each row for rows 2–4 to help with this. (See opposite.)

Using a size G hook and taupe yarn, ch 25, then crochet the following:

Row 1: Starting in the 2nd ch from the hook, sc 24. Ch 1 and turn. {24}

Row 2: Sc 24 across, ch 1, and turn. {24}

Row 3: Skip the first sc, sc 22, sl st, ch 1, and turn. {22}

Row 4: In front loops only, skip the first sc, sc 20, sl st, ch 1, and turn. {20}

Row 5: Sc 2 in the first sc, sc 3, sc 2 in next stitch, sc 10, sc 2 in next stitch, sc 3, sc 2 in next stitch. Ch 1 and turn. {24}

Row 6: Sc 2 in one stitch, sc 5, sc 2 in next stitch, sc 10, sc 2 in next stitch, sc 5, sc 2 in next stitch. Ch 1 and turn. {28}

Row 7: Sc 2 in one stitch, sc 26, sc 2 in next stitch. Ch 1 and turn. {30}

Rows 8–10: Sc 30 across. Ch 1 and turn at the ends of rows 8–9. At the end of row 10, fasten off and weave in the end. {30}

Fold coat at the line of stitches in the front loops to create the Inverness cape over his coat and, using a length of taupe yarn and a tapestry needle, sew the midpoint of the coat collar to the back of his neck with a few stitches. Thread a short length of black lightweight yarn or embroidery floss between the two points where the coat meets, at Sherlock's neck. Pull the two ends through evenly and tie a bow. Trim excess.

Some of the characters in this book wear jackets, and part of their instructions look like this:

Row 3: Skip the first sc, sc 28, sl st in last stitch, ch1, and turn. {28}

This visual guide explains it all. We'll start at the end of the row, where the directions say "sl st in the last stitch, ch 1, and turn." Here is the last single crochet stitch in the row, indicated by a pink stitch marker.

Insert the hook into the next stitch, yarn over, and pull up a slip stitch.

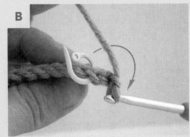

Then ch 1, and turn your work around.

Now let's move on to the beginning of the next row, where the directions say "Skip the first sc, then sc __." When you've turned the work around, the last single crochet stitch you made is now the first one in the row. Skip past the first single crochet stitch (do not count the chain or slip stitches), and insert the hook under the next stitch to make the first single crochet stitch in the new row (C). This is where the stitch marker comes in handy to show where to skip over.

Move the stitch marker onto the new first single crochet stitch of the row and continue to crochet across as normal (D).

"'I wear the chain I forged in life,' replied the Ghost. 'I made it link by link, and yard by yard; I girded it on of my own free will, and of my own free will I wore it. Is its pattern strange to you? If so, don't be afraid to ask an experienced crocheter for help.'"

EBENEZER SCROOGE

CHARLES DICKENS'S *A CHRISTMAS CAROL*, 1843

If Ebenezer Scrooge were to live through Christmas today, he'd be as grumpy as ever. The endless holiday songs on the radio, the fights over that perfect gift, the awkward gift exchanges at the office . . . I feel you, Mr. Scrooge. Christmas is kind of a holiday circus.

MATERIALS

- Size E and size G crochet hooks
- Worsted-weight yarn in silver gray, cream, white, deep green, and red
- 6-mm black plastic safety eyes
- Tapestry needle
- 7" length of 18-gauge aluminum, or other silver-colored wire
- Pencil
- Fiberfill
- Polypellets, optional
- 1/8"-wide gold ribbon, optional

NOTES

Use a size E crochet hook for all parts unless otherwise specified.

Work in continuous rounds unless otherwise specified.

HEAD

Round 1: Starting with silver-gray yarn, sc 5 in magic ring. {5}

Round 2: [Sc 2 in one stitch] 5 times. {10}

Round 3: [Sc 2 in one stitch] 10 times. {20}

Round 4: [Sc 3, sc 2 in next stitch] 5 times. {25}

Round 5: [Sc 4, sc 2 in next stitch] 5 times. {30}

Round 6: [Sc 9, sc 2 in next stitch] 3 times, changing to cream yarn in the last stitch. {33}

Rounds 7–9: Sc 14, changing to silver-gray yarn, sc 19, changing to cream yarn. {14 cream + 19 silver gray = 33}

Round 10: Sc 9, dec 1, sc 3, changing to silver-gray yarn. Sc 6, dec 1, sc 9, dec 1, changing to cream yarn. {13 cream + 17 silver-gray = 30}

Round 11: [Sc 4, dec 1] twice, sc 1, changing to silver-gray yarn. Sc 3, dec 1, [sc 4, dec 1] twice, changing to cream yarn in the last stitch. {11 cream + 14 silver-gray = 25}

Round 12: [Sc 3, dec 1] twice, sc 1, changing to silver-gray yarn. Sc 2, dec 1, [sc 3, dec 1] twice, changing to cream yarn in the last stitch. {9 cream + 11 silver-gray = 20}

Round 13: [Sc 2, dec 1] twice, sc 1, changing to silver-gray yarn. Sc 1, dec 1, [sc 2, dec 1] twice. {7 cream + 8 silver-gray = 15}

Fasten off and tuck in the end. Attach eyes between rows 8 and 9 (two rows below the hairline), approximately 6 stitches apart. Using overlapping straight stitches of silver-gray yarn and a tapestry needle, sew on two grumpy eyebrows.

MUTTONCHOPS (MAKE 2)

Using silver-gray yarn, ch 6 and crochet the following:

Row 1: Starting in the 2nd ch from the hook, sc 5 across. {5}

Fasten off, leaving a tail for sewing, and use a tapestry needle to sew one muttonchop onto each side of his face.

GLASSES

Wrap a 7-inch length of 18-gauge wire around a pencil, leaving about 1½ to 2 inches unwrapped (A). This will become one lens of Scrooge's glasses.

Place the loop over one eye. Use the pencil again to make a second loop that will align with the other eye. Bend down the ends of the wire at a 90-degree angle and insert them at eye level into his head (B).

Secure the glasses by bending the ends of wire inside the head to lie flat.

Optional: Sew a few stitches to secure the ends inside the head. Shift the glasses below his eyes to make him look down in contempt. Stuff head firmly with fiberfill.

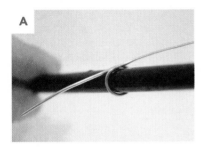

PAJAMAS

Using a size G hook and white yarn, ch 15, then sl st into the first chain to form a ring.

Round 1: Sc 15. {15}

Round 2: [Sc 2, sc 2 in next stitch] 5 times. {20}

Round 3: [Sc 1, sc 2 in next stitch] 10 times. {30}

Rounds 4–7: Sc 30. {30}

Round 8: [Sc 5, sc 2 in next stitch] 5 times. {35}

Fasten off and weave in the end.

BODY

Using white yarn, crochet a Basic Body as on page 11. Fasten off, leaving a tail for sewing.

Stuff the body firmly with fiberfill, or fill with polypellets first and then top off with fiberfill. Place pajamas on body, lining up the stitches along the neckline; sew head, pajamas, and body together using a whipstitch.

HAT

Round 1: With white yarn, sc 3 in magic ring. {3}

Round 2: In back loops only, sc 3. {3}

Round 3: [Sc 2 in one stitch] 3 times. {6}

Round 4: [Sc 1, sc 2 in next stitch] 3 times. {9}

Round 5: Sc 9. {9}

Round 6: [Sc 2, sc 2 in next stitch] 3 times. {12}

Rounds 7–8: Sc 12. {12}

Round 9: [Sc 3, sc 2 in next stitch] 3 times. {15}

Round 10: Sc 15. {15}

Round 11: [Sc 2, sc 2 in next stitch] 5 times. {20}

Round 12: [Sc 3, sc 2 in next stitch] 5 times. {25}

Round 13: [Sc 4, sc 2 in next stitch] 5 times. {30}

Round 14: Sc 30. {30}

Fasten off, leaving a tail for sewing. Sew hat onto head using only the inner ring of loops only (back loops). Fold over the tip of the hat as desired.

WREATH

Using a size G hook and deep-green yarn, ch 26, then crochet the following:

Row 1: Starting in the 2nd ch from the hook, [sc 1, ch 2, then sl st in the front two loops of the previous sc, sl st in the next ch] repeatedly down the chain.

Fasten off, leaving a short tail.

Using red yarn and a tapestry needle, sew onto the wreath a few French knots (see tutorial, opposite) as holly berries. Encircle Scrooge's neck with the wreath and tie ends together. Weave in the ends. You may further secure the wreath with a single stitch of yarn at the back of the neck. Optional: Tie on a gold ribbon bow for extra (grumpy) cheer.

French knots are great for adding little dots onto your projects. They could be buttons, eyes, or in Scrooge's case berries on a festive wreath. Here's how to make them.

1 Pull a length of yarn or thread out of your fabric.

2 Wrap the yarn or thread around the needle 3 or 4 times.

3 Reinsert the needle close to the yarn's original exit point, but not exactly at the same place.

4 Holding the yarn closest to the eye of the needle with one hand and the end of your needle with the other, carefully pull the needle through, but not all the way. Stop when the knot is the size you want it and then tie it off. To make larger dots, wrap the yarn or thread around the needle more than 3 or 4 times.

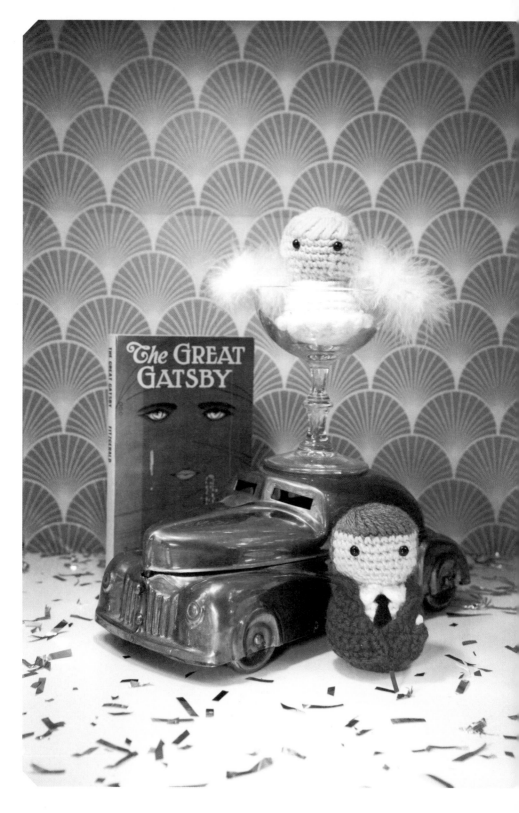

"'Can't repeat the past?' he cried incredulously. 'Why of course you can! Just follow the pattern and do everything in square brackets as many times as it requires.'"

JAY GATSBY AND DAISY BUCHANAN

F. SCOTT FITZGERALD'S *THE GREAT GATSBY*, 1925

The 1920s were a glamorous time, and Jay Gatsby spared no expense in throwing the most lavish parties, hoping to catch the eye and win the heart of Daisy Buchanan, the love of his life. But the great American novel about hopes, dreams, and a creepy billboard is a cautionary tale that all that glitters isn't gold.

MATERIALS

- Size E crochet hook
- 6-mm black plastic safety eyes
- Tapestry needle
- Fiberfill
- Polypellets, optional

FOR DAISY:
- Worsted weight yarn in canary yellow, cream, and white
- Approximately 7"-length thin beading wire
- Pearl seed beads
- Crimping bead
- Pliers
- Scissors
- White sewing thread and sewing needle
- Approximately 7½"-long small white crafting feather boa (if a small feather boa is unavailable, try white eyelash yarn)
- Sticky gems, optional (about 3 mm)

FOR JAY:
- Worsted weight yarn in sand, cream, navy blue, and white
- Paper and pencil
- Black and white felt
- Hot-glue gun
- Straight pins

NOTES

Work in continuous rounds unless otherwise specified.

DAISY BUCHANAN

HEAD

Round 1: Starting with canary-yellow yarn, sc 5 in magic ring. {5}

Round 2: [Sc 2 in one stitch] 5 times. {10}

Round 3: [Sc 2 in one stitch] 10 times. {20}

Round 4: [Sc 3, sc 2 in next stitch] 5 times. {25}

Round 5: [Sc 4, sc 2 in next stitch] 5 times, changing to cream yarn in the last stitch. {30}

Round 6: Sc 9, sc 2 in next stitch, sc 3, changing to canary-yellow yarn. Sc 6, sc 2 in next stitch, sc 9, sc 2 in next stitch, changing to cream yarn. {14 cream + 19 canary-yellow = 33}

Rounds 7–9: Sc 14, changing to canary-yellow yarn, sc 19, changing to cream yarn. {14 cream + 19 canary-yellow = 33}

Round 10: Sc 9, dec 1, sc 3, changing to canary-yellow yarn. Sc 6, dec 1, sc 9, dec 1, changing to cream yarn. {13 cream + 17 canary-yellow = 30}

Round 11: [Sc 4, dec 1] twice, sc 1, changing to canary-yellow yarn. Sc 3, dec 1, [sc 4, dec 1] twice, changing to cream yarn in the last stitch. {11 cream + 14 canary-yellow = 25}

Round 12: [Sc 3, dec 1] twice, sc 1, changing to canary-yellow yarn. Sc 2, dec 1, [sc 3, dec 1] twice, changing to cream yarn in the last stitch. {9 cream + 11 canary-yellow = 20}

Round 13: [Sc 2, dec 1] twice, sc 1, changing to canary-yellow yarn. Sc 1, dec 1, [sc 2, dec 1] twice. {7 cream + 8 canary-yellow = 15}

Fasten off and tuck in end. Attach eyes between rows 8 and 9 (three rows below the hairline), approximately 6 stitches apart.

HAIR DETAIL

Using canary-yellow yarn, sew a row of sideswept bangs across Daisy's forehead. (See page 12.) Thread a length of canary-yellow yarn onto a tapestry needle and bring it up at her right temple (your left if facing her; A) and back down at a point in her cheek, but don't pull the yarn too taut (B). Bring the needle back up in the stitch next to the previous point at her temple.

Reinsert the needle into the same spot on her cheek as before, and bring out the needle pointed away from her cheek at a spot between the two ends of the previous stitches (C) to create a midpoint anchor for a crescent-shaped curve.

Bring the needle back into the same anchoring point to form a single stitch and secure the two cresent-shaped strands (D).

Stuff head firmly with fiberfill.

BODY

Using white yarn, crochet a Basic Body as on page 11. Fasten off, leaving a tail for sewing.

SKIRT DETAIL

Hold the body upside down and look for the "skip" on the row of stitches in the back loops. This will be the back of Daisy's body. Starting 2 rows from skip, create a surface chain around the body using white yarn. It will total 25 stitches. (See page 13 for more on creating a surface chain.)

surface chain

Then continue to use the white yarn to crochet the following repeatedly along the chain until you make a full round:

[Sc 1, dc 1, sc 1] in one stitch, sl st in next stitch.

Stuff the body firmly with fiberfill, or fill with polypellets first and then top off with fiberfill. Sew on the head using a whipstitch.

NECKLACE

String about 4$\frac{1}{2}$ inches of pearl seed beads onto the beading wire. Place the beaded wire around her neck and thread the ends through a crimping bead and through a few beads on each side (A).

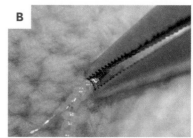

Pull the ends of the wire until the beads come together and squeeze the crimping bead flat with pliers (B).

Trim excess wire with scissors. Optional: Use white sewing thread to secure the necklace to the back of her neck with a single stitch.

FINISHING TOUCHES

Sew feather boa to Daisy's neck with a few stitches of white sewing thread. (Alternatively, ch 35 with white eyelash yarn, fasten off, and sew onto Daisy's neck.)

Place sticky gems at the troughs of the scalloping on Daisy's skirt to make her sparkle!

JAY GATSBY

HEAD

Round 1: Starting with sand yarn, sc 5 in magic ring. {5}

Round 2: [Sc 2 in one stitch] 5 times. {10}

Round 3: [Sc 2 in one stitch] 10 times. {20}

Round 4: [Sc 3, sc 2 in next stitch] 5 times. {25}

Round 5: [Sc 4, sc 2 in next stitch] 5 times. {30}

Round 6: [Sc 9, sc 2 in next stitch] 3 times, changing to cream yarn in the last stitch. {33}

Rounds 7–9: Sc 14, changing to sand yarn, sc 19, changing to cream yarn. {14 cream + 19 sand = 33}

Round 10: Sc 9, dec 1, sc 3, changing to sand yarn. Sc 6, dec 1, sc 9, dec 1, changing to cream yarn. {13 cream + 17 sand = 30}

Round 11: [Sc 4, dec 1] twice, sc 1, changing to sand yarn. Sc 3, dec 1, [sc 4, dec 1] twice, changing to cream yarn in the last stitch. {11 cream + 14 sand = 25}

Round 12: [Sc 3, dec 1] twice, sc 1, changing to sand yarn. Sc 2, dec 1, [sc 3, dec 1] twice, changing to cream yarn in the last stitch. {9 cream + 11 sand = 20}

Round 13: [Sc 2, dec 1] twice, sc 1, changing to sand yarn. Sc 1, dec 1, [sc 2, dec 1] twice. {7 cream + 8 sand = 15}

Fasten off and tuck in the end. Attach eyes between rows 8 and 9 (two rows below the hairline), approximately 6 stitches apart.

Using sand yarn, sew a row of combed-back hair along Gatsby's hairline. (See page 12 for instructions.)

Stuff head firmly with fiberfill.

BODY

Starting with navy-blue yarn, crochet a Basic Body as on page 11, changing to white yarn in the last stitch of round 8. Fasten off, leaving a tail for sewing.

Stuff the body firmly with fiberfill, or fill with polypellets first and then top off with fiberfill. Sew on the head using a whipstitch.

COLLAR TIPS (MAKE 2)

Using white yarn, ch 4, then crochet the following:

Row 1: Starting in the 2nd ch from the hook, sc 1, hdc 1, ch 1, and sl st in the front two loops of the previous hdc, then sl st in the next ch.

Fasten off, leaving a tail for sewing. This should result in a small triangle. Position collar tips on Gatsby's neck and sew in place with yarn tails and a tapestry needle. Draw onto a piece of paper a necktie shape (like the one below) to fit Gatsby's shirt; cut it out. Place pattern on black felt and cut around the shape to make a small black tie. Hot-glue tie underneath the two collar flaps.

JACKET

Work from the bottom hem up to the collar. Do not count slip stitches in your stitch count for this portion. Use stitch markers to mark the first and last sc of each row. (See page 43.)

Using navy-blue yarn, ch 31, then crochet the following:

Row 1: Starting in the 2nd ch from the hook, sc 30 across, ch 1, and turn. {30}

Row 2: Sc 30, ch 1, and turn {30}

Row 3: Skip the first sc, then sc 28, sl st in last stitch, ch 1, and turn. {28}

Row 4: Skip the first sc, then sc 26, sl st in last stitch, ch 1, and turn. {26}

Row 5: Skip the first sc, then sc 24, sl st in last stitch, ch 1, and turn. {24}

Row 6: Skip the first sc, then sc 22, sl st in last stitch, ch 1, and turn. {22}

Row 7: Skip the first sc, then sc 20, sl st in last stitch, ch 1, and turn. {20}

Row 8: Skip the first sc, then sc 18, sl st in last stitch. {18}

Fasten off and weave in the end.

Fold down the top row (the shortest row) of the jacket to create a collar/lapel and position it over the body. Pin it in place while you determine the best position for the pocket and pocket square.

POCKET AND POCKET SQUARE

Using navy-blue yarn, ch 3, then crochet the following:

Row 1: Starting in the 2nd ch from the hook, sc 2. Fasten off, leaving a tail for sewing.

Cut a small piece of white felt and place underneath the pocket before sewing it on. Position the pocket on the front of Gatsby's jacket, then remove the jacket and sew on the pocket.

Use a length of navy-blue yarn to secure the jacket to Gatsby's body. Attach with stitches on both sides and on the back of the neck. Sew a stitch through both layers of the jacket at the front to close it. (Alternatively, use hot glue to close jacket.)

"But this has been amigurumi of passion, not of principle, nor even purpose."

HESTER PRYNNE

NATHANIEL HAWTHORNE'S *THE SCARLET LETTER: A ROMANCE*, 1850

Sin was a big deal among the Puritans of colonial America. After becoming pregnant out of wedlock, Hester Prynne was doomed to wear a mark of shame for life. Rumors about her who's-the-baby-daddy scandal would have spread like wildfire on Facebook, so maybe modern shaming isn't much different from the old days.

MATERIALS

- Size E and size H crochet hooks
- Worsted-weight yarn in cream, brown, and white
- 6-mm black plastic safety eyes
- Fiberfill
- Tapestry needle
- Polypellets, optional
- 5" x 1¹/₄" piece white felt
- White sewing thread and needle, or hot-glue gun
- Red embroidery floss and embroidery needle

NOTES

Use a size E crochet hook for all parts unless otherwise specified.

Work in continuous rounds unless otherwise specified.

59

HEAD

Round 1: Starting with brown yarn, sc 5 in magic ring. {5}

Round 2: [Sc 2 in one stitch] 5 times. {10}

Round 3: [Sc 2 in one stitch] 10 times. {20}

Round 4: [Sc 3, sc 2 in next stitch] 5 times. {25}

Round 5: [Sc 4, sc 2 in next stitch] 5 times. {30}

Round 6: [Sc 9, sc 2 in next stitch] 3 times, changing to cream yarn in the last stitch. {33}

Rounds 7–9: Sc 14, changing to brown yarn, sc 19, changing to cream yarn. {14 cream + 19 brown = 33}

Round 10: Sc 9, dec 1, sc 3, changing to brown yarn. Sc 6, dec 1, sc 9, dec 1, changing to cream yarn. {13 cream + 17 brown = 30}

Round 11: [Sc 4, dec 1] twice, sc 1, changing to brown yarn. Sc 3, dec 1, [sc 4, dec 1] twice, changing to cream yarn in the last stitch. {11 cream + 14 brown = 25}

Round 12: [Sc 3, dec 1] twice, sc 1, changing to brown yarn. Sc 2, dec 1, [sc 3, dec 1] twice, changing to cream yarn in the last stitch. {9 cream + 11 brown = 20}

Round 13: [Sc 2, dec 1] twice, sc 1, changing to brown yarn. Sc 1, dec 1, [sc 2, dec 1] twice. {7 cream + 8 brown = 15}

Fasten off and tuck in the end. Attach eyes between rows 8 and 9 (two rows below the hairline), approximately 6 stitches apart. Stuff head firmly with fiberfill.

HAIR BUN

Round 1: With brown yarn, sc 5 in magic ring. {5}

Round 2: [Sc 2 in one stitch] 5 times. {10}

Round 3: Sc 10. {10}

Round 4: Dec 5. {5}

Fasten off, leaving a tail for sewing. Sew to the back of Hester's head.

BODY

Using brown yarn, crochet a Basic Body as on page 11. Fasten off and leave a tail for sewing.

SKIRT

Hold the body upside down and look for the "skip" on the row of stitches in the back loops. This will be the back of Hester's body. Using brown yarn, start 3 rows from skip and create a surface chain around the body. It will total 25 stitches. (See page 13 for more on creating a surface chain.)

Continue to use the brown yarn to crochet the following along the surface chain:

Rows 1–3: Sc 25. {25}

Row 4: [Sc 1, sc 2 in next stitch] repeatedly until you reach the end, then fasten off.

Stuff the body firmly with fiberfill, or fill with polypellets first and then top off with fiberfill. Sew to the head using a whipstitch.

COLLAR

Using a size H hook and white yarn, loosely ch 17, then crochet the following:

Row 1: Starting in the 3rd ch from the hook, hdc 15 times across. {15}

Fasten off and leave a tail for sewing. Using the length of yarn at the end, sew on to Hester's neck.

FINISHING TOUCHES

Thread an 8-inch length of white yarn through the base of her head, using the points where the color changes from her face to her hair as the entry and exit points (A).

Pull the yarn so the two ends are of equal length. Bring the ends to the center and tie a bow in the middle under her chin (B).

Wrap the felt rectangle over Hester's head. Secure the short sides to the base of the head with stitches or hot glue.

Finally, using red embroidery floss, stitch a letter "A" onto Hester's chest.

"Oh, why am I not of yarn, like you?"

QUASIMODO AND ESMERALDA

VICTOR HUGO'S *THE HUNCHBACK OF NOTRE-DAME*, 1831

The Hunchback of Notre-Dame is a pretty juicy story. Love, lust, betrayal, attempted murder, actual murder, public humiliation, executions—it has all the ingredients for a tragedy that could rival some of today's best dramatic television.

MATERIALS

- Size E crochet hook
- 6-mm black plastic safety eyes
- Fiberfill
- Tapestry needle
- Polypellets

FOR QUASIMODO:
- Worsted-weight yarn in light brown, cream, black, and olive green
- Hemp cord
- Brown sewing thread and sewing needle, optional

FOR ESMERALDA:
- Worsted-weight yarn in black, caramel, peacock blue, white, marigold, rust, and plum

- Ribbon or cord of your choice for hair band
- Hot-glue gun, optional
- 2 gold jump rings (about 10 mm diameter)
- Sewing thread and needle
- Green bead
- Approximately 7"-long thin brown cord
- Embroidery floss (color of your choice) and embroidery needle, optional

NOTES

Work in continuous rounds unless otherwise specified.

The sky's the limit when it comes to Esmeralda's clothing. You can use any combination of colors for her skirt, top, and sarong, and the sarong can be embellished with embroidery or beading. You can use small charms instead of jump rings for earrings, or braid colorful cords to make her hair band. Make her as lively and spirited as you see fit!

QUASIMODO

HEAD

Round 1: Starting with light-brown yarn, sc 5 in magic ring. {5}

Round 2: [Sc 2 in one stitch] 5 times. {10}

Round 3: [Sc 2 in one stitch] 10 times. {20}

Round 4: [Sc 3, sc 2 in next stitch] 5 times. {25}

Round 5: [Sc 4, sc 2 in next stitch] 5 times. {30}

Round 6: [Sc 9, sc 2 in next stitch] 3 times, changing to cream yarn in the last stitch. {33}

Rounds 7–9: Sc 14, changing to light-brown yarn, sc 19, changing to cream yarn. {14 cream + 19 light-brown = 33}

Round 10: Sc 9, dec 1, sc 3, changing to light-brown yarn. Sc 6, dec 1, sc 9, dec 1, changing to cream yarn. {13 cream + 17 light-brown = 30}

Round 11: [Sc 4, dec 1] twice, sc 1, changing to light-brown yarn. Sc 3, dec 1, [sc 4, dec 1] twice, changing to cream yarn in the last stitch. {11 cream + 14 light-brown = 25}

Round 12: [Sc 3, dec 1] twice, sc 1, changing to light-brown yarn. Sc 2, dec 1, [sc 3, dec 1] twice, changing to cream yarn in the last stitch. {9 cream + 11 light-brown = 20}

Attach eyes between rows 8 and 9 (2 rows below the hairline), approximately 6 stitches apart. Stuff head firmly with fiberfill.

Round 13: Dec 10. {10}

Round 14: Dec 5. {5}

Fasten off and close off the head (see page 9 for instructions). To make Quasimodo's drooping eyelid, thread a tapestry needle with cream yarn. Bring needle and yarn out on one side of one eye and reinsert the needle on the other side (A). Don't pull too taut.

Bring needle back out at a spot immediately above his eye (B).

Reinsert the needle at the point above his eye to anchor the curve (C). Then bring the needle back out at the point next to his eye. Pull through to make a curve (D).

Repeat through the same sewing points to make a second layer.

BODY

Work from bottom up.

Round 1: Starting with black yarn, sc 5 in magic ring. {5}

Round 2: [Sc 2 in one stitch] 5 times. {10}

Round 3: [Sc 1, sc 2 in next stitch] 5 times. {15}

Round 4: [Sc 2, sc 2 in next stitch] 5 times. {20}

Round 5: [Sc 3, sc 2 in next stitch] 5 times. {25}

Round 6: [Sc 4, sc 2 in next stitch] 5 times. {30}

Round 7: [Sc 5, sc 2 in next stitch] 5 times. {35}

Round 8: In back loops only, sc 35. {35}

Rounds 9–10: Sc 35, changing to olive-green yarn in the last stitch of Round 10. {35}

Rounds 11–14: Sc 35. {35}

Round 15: [Sc 5, dec 1] 5 times. {30}

Round 16: [Sc 8, dec 1] 3 times. {27}

Round 17: [Sc 7, dec 1] 3 times. {24}

Round 18: [Sc 6, dec 1] 3 times. {21}

Round 19: [Sc 5, dec 1] 3 times. {18}

Fill body with polypellets and top off with fiberfill.

Round 20: [Sc 1, dec 1] 6 times. {12}

Round 21: Dec 6 times. {6}

Fasten off, close off the body, and tuck in the end.

TUNIC

Hold body upside down. Still using olive-green yarn, create a surface chain starting at the point where the color change between the black and olive-green yarn begins. (It will total 35 stitches; see page 13.) Continue to use olive-green yarn to crochet the following along surface chain:

Round 1: Sc 35. {35}

Fasten off and weave in the end.

FINISHING TOUCHES

Using a length of light-brown yarn and a tapestry needle, sew the back of Quasimodo's head to the body, about one-third down from the top of the hump.

Tie a 16-inch length of hemp cord around his waist. Trim excess. Optional: Secure the cord with a few stitches of brown thread.

ESMERALDA

HEAD

Round 1: Starting with black yarn, sc 5 in magic ring. {5}

Round 2: [Sc 2 in one stitch] 5 times. {10}

Round 3: [Sc 2 in one stitch] 10 times. {20}

Round 4: [Sc 3, Sc 2 in next stitch] 5 times. {25}

Round 5: [Sc 4, Sc 2 in next stitch] 5 times, changing to caramel yarn in the last stitch. {30}

Round 6: Sc 9, sc 2 in next stitch, sc 3, changing to black yarn. Sc 6, sc 2 in next stitch, sc 9, sc 2 in next stitch, changing to caramel yarn. {14 caramel + 19 black = 33}

Rounds 7–9: Sc 14, changing to black yarn, sc 19, changing to caramel yarn. {14 caramel + 19 black = 33}

Round 10: Sc 9, dec 1, sc 3, changing to black yarn. Sc 6, dec 1, sc 9, dec 1, changing to caramel yarn. {13 caramel + 17 black = 30}

Round 11: [Sc 4, dec 1] twice, sc 1, changing to black yarn. Sc 3, dec 1, [sc 4, dec 1] twice, changing to caramel yarn in the last stitch. {11 caramel + 14 black = 25}

Round 12: [Sc 3, dec 1] twice, sc 1, changing to black yarn. Sc 2, dec 1, [sc 3, dec 1] twice, changing to caramel yarn in the last stitch. {9 caramel + 11 black = 20}

Round 13: [Sc 2, dec 1] twice, sc 1, changing to black yarn. Sc 1, dec 1, [sc 2, dec 1] twice. {7 caramel + 8 black = 15}

Fasten off and tuck in the end. Attach eyes between rows 8 and 9 (three rows below the hairline), approximately 6 stitches apart.

Using black yarn, sew a row of sideswept bangs across Esmeralda's forehead (see page 12). Then make the rest of her hair by hooking several 6-inch strands of black yarn all around the head using cow hitch knots (see page 11). Manually split the strands to make hair more voluminous and lively, then trim to your liking. Stuff head firmly with fiberfill.

BODY

Starting with peacock-blue yarn, crochet a Basic Body as on page 11, changing to white yarn in the last stitch of round 8. Fasten off, leaving a tail for sewing.

SKIRT

Hold the body upside down and, using peacock-blue yarn, create a surface chain starting at the point where the color change between the blue and white yarn begins. (It will total 25 stitches.) Along the surface chain:

Round 1: Sc 25. {25}

Round 2: [Sc 4, sc 2 in next stitch] 5 times. {30}

Round 3: Sc 30, changing to marigold yarn. {30}

Round 4: Sc 30, changing to peacock blue yarn. {30}

Round 5: [Sc 1, hdc 1, sc 1] in one stitch, sl st in next stitch. Repeat 15 times. Fasten off and weave in the end.

Using rust yarn, sew a line of backstitches along the edge of the skirt where the marigold yarn meets the blue yarn. Stuff body firmly with fiberfill, or fill with polypellets first and then top off with fiberfill. Sew on the head using a whipstitch.

FINISHING TOUCHES

Hair band: Separate one section of Esmeralda's hair at the hairline from the rest. Wrap the ribbon around the separated section and bring the ends of the ribbon together at the nape of her neck.

Tie ends together or secure with hot glue. Replace the separated section of hair across her forehead.

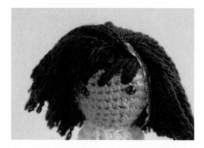

Earrings: Using sewing thread, sew a jump ring to each side of her head.

Sarong: Using plum yarn, leave a 2-inch starting tail, then ch 26. Crochet the following:

Row 1: Starting in the 2nd ch from the hook, sc 25 across. Ch 1 and turn. {25}

Row 2: Sc 5, dc 5, tr 5, dc 5, sc 5. {25}

Fasten off and leave a 2-inch tail.

Cut 25 2-inch pieces of plum yarn. Hook each strand along the edge of the sarong using cow hitch knots (see page 11) to create a row of tassels. Trim ends if necessary. If desired, you may embroider details onto the sarong (I used gold embroidery floss). Wrap the sarong around Esmeralda's waist and tie it off to the side. You may either sew the sarong to her waist with a few stitches of plum yarn or leave it unsecured to make it removable.

Necklace: Thread a green bead onto brown cord, and tie around Esmeralda's neck. Trim excess cord.

"Call me Ishmael. Some years ago—never mind how long precisely—having little or no money in my purse, and nothing particular to interest me, I thought I would take up crochet."

CAPTAIN AHAB AND MOBY DICK

HERMAN MELVILLE'S *MOBY-DICK*, 1851

We get it, Captain. You lost your leg to a white whale and became obsessed with seeking revenge. Everyone has bad relationships, and love hurts, but sometimes you just have to let things go. There's also that tiny detail of the whale being 400 times your size. Just saying that you might want to account for these things before embarking on a lifelong rampage.

MATERIALS

- Tapestry needle
- Fiberfill

FOR AHAB:
- Size E crochet hook
- Worsted weight yarn in silver gray, cream, black, brown, and light blue
- 6-mm black plastic safety eyes
- Cream embroidery floss and embroidery needle
- Disposable chopstick
- Knife or heavy-duty scissors

- Polypellets, optional
- Straight pins
- 4½" × 2" piece of black felt
- Black thread and sewing needle

FOR MOBY DICK:
- Size G or H crochet hook
- Worsted-weight yarn in white
- 9-mm black plastic safety eyes
- Closing stitch marker or safety pin, optional

NOTES

Work in continuous rounds unless otherwise specified.

AHAB

HEAD

Round 1: Starting with silver-gray yarn, sc 5 in magic ring. {5}

Round 2: [Sc 2 in one stitch] 5 times. {10}

Round 3: [Sc 2 in one stitch] 10 times. {20}

Round 4: [Sc 3, sc 2 in next stitch] 5 times. {25}

Round 5: [Sc 4, sc 2 in next stitch] 5 times. {30}

Round 6: [Sc 9, sc 2 in next stitch] 3 times, changing to cream yarn in the last stitch. {33}

Rounds 7–9: Sc 14, changing to silver-gray yarn, sc 19, changing to cream yarn. {14 cream + 19 silver-gray = 33}

Round 10: Sc 9, dec 1, sc 3, changing to silver-gray yarn. Sc 6, dec 1, sc 9, dec 1, changing to cream yarn. {13 cream + 17 silver-gray = 30}

Round 11: [Sc 4, dec 1] twice, sc 1, changing to silver-gray yarn. Sc 3, dec 1, [sc 4, dec 1] twice, changing to cream yarn in the last stitch. {11 cream + 14 silver-gray = 25}

Round 12: [Sc 3, dec 1] twice, sc 1, changing to silver-gray yarn. Sc 2, dec 1, [sc 3, dec 1] twice, changing to cream yarn in the last stitch. {9 cream + 11 silver-gray = 20}

Round 13: [Sc 2, dec 1] twice, sc 1, changing to silver-gray yarn. Sc 1, dec 1, [sc 2, dec 1] twice. {7 cream + 8 silver-gray = 15}

Fasten off and tuck in the end. Attach eyes between rows 8 and 9 (two rows below the hairline), approximately 6 stitches apart.

Using overlapping straight stitches of silver-gray yarn and a tapestry needle, sew on two angry eyebrows. The man's got a lifelong grudge; he's going to be perpetually mad! Using cream embroidery floss, sew a scar onto his face.

BEARD AND SIDEBURNS

Captain Ahab's beard and sideburns will be made in one continuous piece.

Using silver-gray yarn, ch 21, then crochet the following:

Row 1: Starting in the 2nd ch from the hook, sc 6, dc 8, sc 6. {20}

Fasten off and leave a tail for sewing.

To sew the beard and sideburns onto Ahab's face, line up the foundation chain of the piece with the sides of his face and the second-to-last row of the head. Sew only along the foundation chain side to attach the beard, and sew down both the foundation chain side and the crocheted side to attach the sideburns. Stuff head firmly with fiberfill.

HAT

Round 1: With black yarn, sc 5 in magic ring. {5}

Round 2: [Sc 2 in one stitch] 5 times. {10}

Round 3: [Sc 1, sc 2 in next stitch] 5 times. {15}

Round 4: [Sc 2, sc 2 in next stitch] 5 times. {20}

Round 5: [Sc 3, sc 2 in next stitch] 5 times. {25}

Round 6: [Sc 4, sc 2 in next stitch] 5 times. {30}

Round 7: [Sc 5, sc 2 in next stitch] 5 times. {35}

Round 8: [Sc 6, sc 2 in next stitch] 5 times. {40}

Round 9: Sc 40. {40}

Round 10: [Sc 6, dec 1] 5 times. {35}

Round 11: In front loops only: Sc 2, dc 10, sc 2, sl st and fasten off.

If you want to sew his hat to his head, leave a tail and sew in place. Otherwise, cut the yarn and weave in the end.

BODY

Note: Captain Ahab's peg leg is held in place only by tension. If you wish to make an Ahab that can be handled and played with, instead of solely for display, crochet a Basic Body as on page 11, changing from brown to light blue at the end of round 8.

Work from bottom up.

Round 1: Starting with brown yarn, sc 5 in magic ring. {5}

Round 2: [Sc 2 in one stitch] 5 times. {10}

Round 3: [Sc 1, sc 2 in next stitch] 5 times. {15}

Round 4: [Sc 2, sc 2 in next stitch] 5 times. {20}

Round 5: [Sc 3, sc 2 in next stitch] 5 times. {25}

Round 6: In back loops only, sc 25, changing to light-blue yarn. {25}

Rounds 7–9: Sc 25. {25}

Round 10: [Sc 3, dec 1] 5 times. {20}

Round 11: [Sc 2, dec 1] 5 times. {15}

Fasten off, leaving a tail for sewing.

LEG

Round 1: Starting with black yarn, sc in magic ring. {6}

Round 2: [Sc 2 in one stitch] 6 times. {12}

Round 3: In back loops only, sc 12, changing to brown yarn in the last stitch. {12}

Round 4: Sc 12. {12}

Fasten off, leaving a tail for sewing. Sew the leg onto one half of the bottom of the body. When you have sewn halfway around the leg, fill it with either fiberfill or polypellets, and then complete sewing.

PEG LEG

Using a knife or scissors, carefully cut an approximately 1½-inch piece from the tip of the chopstick. Insert the piece into the bottom of the body from the inside out, positioning it opposite his leg.

Stuff the body firmly with fiberfill, or fill with polypellets first and then top off with fiberfill. Stuff carefully around the chopstick. Using a whipstitch, sew the head onto the body, being mindful of the placement of the legs.

TRENCH COAT

On the long edge of the felt, fold down ½ inch to form a collar for the coat. Wrap collar around Ahab's neck, pin the coat in place with straight pins, and sew the fold to his neck with a sewing needle and black thread.

MOBY DICK

HEAD AND BODY

Round 1: With white yarn, sc 6 in magic ring. {6}

Round 2: [Sc 2 in one stitch] 6 times. {12}

Round 3: [Sc 1, sc 2 in next stitch] 6 times. {18}

Round 4: [Sc 2, sc 2 in next stitch] 6 times. {24}

Round 5: [Sc 3, sc 2 in next stitch] 6 times. {30}

Round 6: [Sc 4, sc 2 in next stitch] 6 times. {36}

Round 7: [Sc 5, sc 2 in next stitch] 6 times. {42}

Round 8: [Sc 6, sc 2 in next stitch] 6 times. {48}

Round 9: [Sc 7, sc 2 in next stitch] 6 times. {54}

Round 10: [Sc 8, sc 2 in next stitch] 6 times. {60}

Round 11: [Sc 2 in one stitch] twice, sc 58. {62}

Round 12: Sc 1, [sc 2 in one stitch] twice, sc 59. {64}

Round 13: Sc 2, [sc 2 in one stitch] twice, sc 60. {66}

Round 14: Sc 3, [sc 2 in one stitch] twice, sc 61. {68}

Round 15: Sc 4, [sc 2 in one stitch] twice, sc 62. {70}

Round 16: Sc 5, [sc 2 in one stitch] twice, sc 63. {72}

Round 17: Sc 6, [sc 2 in one stitch] twice, sc 64. {74}

Round 18: Sc 6, [sc 2 in one stitch] 4 times, sc 64. {78}

Round 19: Sc 8, [sc 2 in one stitch] 4 times, sc 66. {82}

Round 20: Sc 11, [sc 2 in one stitch] twice, sc 69. {84}

Prior to starting the next round, fold the tail portion of the whale in half and line up stitch #1 with #24, #2 with #23, #3 with #22, and so on, resulting in 12 stitches on each side of the fold (A). You may pin the two sides together with a closing stitch marker or safety pin to keep the stitches aligned.

Crocheting through two stitches at a time (B), sc 11 across to the tip of the whale's tail, then fasten off and use the leftover yarn tail to sew the last two stitches together. Weave in the end.

Round 21: Rejoining the white yarn at the first sc starting from the base of the tail, in back loops only, [sc 8, dec 1] 6 times. {54}

Stuff the tail with a small bit of fiberfill. Attach eyes between rows 18 and 19 (two rows above the ridge formed from crocheting in the back loops only), approximately 12 stitches apart. Resume crocheting in both loops from this point on.

Round 22: [Sc 7, dec 1] 6 times. {48}

Round 23: [Sc 6, dec 1] 6 times. {42}

Round 24: [Sc 5, dec 1] 6 times. {36}

Round 25: [Sc 4, dec 1] 6 times. {30}

Stuff the whale firmly with fiberfill. Continue to stuff as you crochet the rest of the body.

Round 26: [Sc 3, dec 1] 6 times. {24}

Round 27: [Sc 2, dec 1] 6 times. {18}

Round 28: [Sc 1, dec 1] 6 times. {12}

Round 29: Dec 6. {6}

Fasten off and close off the body.

SIDE FINS (MAKE 2)

Round 1: With white yarn, sc 6 in magic ring. {6}

Round 2: [Sc 1, sc 2 in next stitch] 3 times. {9}

Round 3: [Sc 2 in one stitch] 9 times. {18}

Round 4: [Sc 2, sc 2 in next stitch] 6 times. {24}

Rounds 5–6: Sc 24. {24}

Fasten off, leaving a tail for sewing.

For each fin, sew the open end closed using a whipstitch. Then use the remaining length of the yarn tail to sew the sewn-closed edge to the side of the whale, one row above the ridge formed from crocheting in the back loops only.

FLUKE (MAKE 2)

Round 1: With white yarn, sc 4 in magic ring. {4}

Round 2: [Sc 1, sc 2 in next stitch] twice. {6}

Round 3: Sc 6. {6}

Round 4: [Sc 2 in one stitch] 6 times. {12}

Round 5: [Sc 1, sc 2 in next stitch] 6 times. {18}

Rounds 6–7: Sc 18. {18}

Round 8: [Sc 1, dec 1] 6 times. {12}

Round 9: Dec 6 times. {6}

Round 10: Sc 6. {6}

Round 11: [Sc 1, dec 1] twice. {4}

Fasten off and leave a tail for sewing. Close off the end, and flatten each piece into a flat oblong shape. Attach one fluke to each side of the tail tip by sewing halfway up one side of the fluke piece. Weave in the ends.

VARIATIONS

Your whale doesn't have to be monochromatic! Substitute any color for the body, fins, and fluke, switching to white yarn at Round 21 on the body. Baby blue or lavender would be especially cute.

"But am I crocheting too much? People are always telling me I do. Would you rather I didn't crochet? If you say so I'll stop. I can STOP when I make up my mind to it, although it's difficult."

ANNE SHIRLEY

LUCY MAUD MONTGOMERY'S *ANNE OF GREEN GABLES*, 1908

It's Anne with an e, and don't you forget it. Spunky and imaginative, this little red-headed orphan won the hearts of the Cuthberts at Green Gables and became one of the most respected members of the Avonlea community. Just don't call her "Carrots." Ever.

MATERIALS

- Size E crochet hook
- Worsted-weight yarn in rust, cream, olive green, white, and straw
- 6-mm black plastic safety eyes
- Tapestry needle
- Black lightweight yarn (#3) or embroidery floss
- Fiberfill
- Polypellets, optional
- 14"-long, ¹⁄₈"-wide ribbon in a color of your choice
- Hot-glue gun

NOTES

Work in continuous rounds unless otherwise specified.

HEAD

Round 1: Starting with rust yarn, sc 5 in magic ring. {5}

Round 2: [Sc 2 in one stitch] 5 times. {10}

Round 3: [Sc 2 in one stitch] 10 times. {20}

Round 4: [Sc 3, sc 2 in next stitch] 5 times. {25}

Round 5: [Sc 4, sc 2 in next stitch] 5 times, changing to cream yarn in the last stitch. {30}

Round 6: Sc 9, sc 2 in next stitch, sc 3, changing to rust yarn. Sc 6, sc 2 in next stitch, sc 9, sc 2 in next stitch, changing to cream yarn. {14 cream + 19 rust = 33}

Rounds 7–9: Sc 14, changing to rust yarn, sc 19, changing to cream yarn. {14 cream + 19 rust = 33}

Round 10: Sc 9, dec 1, sc 3, changing to rust yarn. Sc 6, dec 1, sc 9, dec 1, changing to cream yarn. {13 cream + 17 rust = 30}

Round 11: [Sc 4, dec 1] twice, sc 1, changing to rust yarn. Sc 3, dec 1, [sc 4, dec 1] twice, changing to cream yarn in the last stitch. {11 cream + 14 rust = 25}

Round 12: [Sc 3, dec 1] twice, sc 1, changing to rust yarn. Sc 2, dec 1, [sc 3, dec 1] twice, changing to cream yarn in the last stitch. {9 cream + 11 rust = 20}

Round 13: [Sc 2, dec 1] twice, sc 1, changing to rust yarn. Sc 1, dec 1, [sc 2, dec 1] twice. {7 cream + 8 rust = 15}

Fasten off and tuck in the end. Attach eyes between rows 8 and 9 (three rows below the hairline), approximately 6 stitches apart.

Using rust yarn, sew a row of sideswept bangs across Anne's forehead (see page 12). Cut six 9-inch strands of rust yarn and make two pigtails (see page 23). Using black lightweight yarn or embroidery floss, tie off pigtails with bows. Stuff head firmly with fiberfill.

BODY

Work from the bottom up.

Round 1: With olive-green yarn, sc 5 in magic ring. {5}

Round 2: [Sc 2 in one stitch] 5 times. {10}

Round 3: [Sc 1, sc 2 in next stitch] 5 times. {15}

Round 4: [Sc 2, sc 2 in next stitch] 5 times. {20}

Round 5: In back loops only, sc 20. {20}

Rounds 6–11: Sc 20. {20}

Round 12: [Sc 2, dec 1] 5 times. {15}

Fasten off, leaving a tail for sewing.

SKIRT

Hold the body upside down and look for the "skip" on the row of stitches in the back loops. This will be the back of Anne's body. Starting 3 rows from the skip, create a surface chain around the body using olive-green yarn. It will total 20 stitches. (See page 13 for creating a surface chain.)

Continue to use the olive-green yarn to crochet the following along the surface chain:

Round 1: Sc 20. {20}

Round 2: [Sc 3, sc 2 in next stitch] 5 times. {25}

Round 3: [Sc 4, sc 2 in next stitch] 5 times {30}

Fasten off and weave in the end.

Stuff the body firmly with fiberfill, or fill with polypellets first and then top off with fiberfill. Sew on the head using a whipstitch.

COLLAR FLAPS (MAKE 2)

Using olive-green yarn, ch 3, then crochet the following:

Row 1: Starting in the 2nd ch from the hook, [sc 1, hdc, sc 1] in one stitch, sl st in last stitch, and fasten off, leaving a tail for sewing.

Sew onto Anne's neck.

PINAFORE

Using white yarn, ch 7, then crochet the following:

Row 1: Starting in the 2nd ch from the hook, sc 6 across. Ch 1 and turn. {6}

Rows 2–3: Sc 6 across. Ch 1 and turn. {6}

Row 4: In back loops only: sc 2 in one stitch, sc 4, sc 2 in one stitch, ch 1 and turn. {8}

Rows 5–6: Sc 8 across. {8}

Fasten off and weave in the ends. Using a length of white yarn, sew the pinafore to the front of Anne's waistline using the unused loops from row 4.

WAISTBAND

Using white yarn, leave a short starting tail for sewing, then ch 18 (this may deviate by a few stitches depending on how tightly you crochet) and fasten off, leaving an end tail for sewing. Sew one of the yarn tails to one side of the waist of Anne's pinafore, then bring the chain around her back and sew the other tail to the other side of the waist.

STRAPS (MAKE 2)

Using white yarn, ch 11, then crochet the following:

Row 1: Starting in the 2nd ch from the hook, sc 10 across, ch 1, and turn. {10}

Complete the following row in the front loops only on one strap and in the back loops only on the other.

Row 2: [Sc 3 in one stitch, sl st in next stitch] 5 times.

Fasten off, leaving a tail for sewing.

Sew straps to the top corners of the pinafore with a tapestry needle, bring them over Anne's shoulders, and arrange the ends in a V at her waistband. Sew in place.

HAT

Round 1: With straw yarn, sc 5 in magic ring. {5}

Round 2: [Sc 2 in one stitch] 5 times. {10}

Round 3: [Sc 1, sc 2 in next stitch] 5 times. {15}

Round 4: [Sc 2, sc 2 in next stitch] 5 times. {20}

Round 5: [Sc 3, sc 2 in next stitch] 5 times. {25}

Round 6: [Sc 4, sc 2 in next stitch] 5 times. {30}

Round 7: [Sc 5, sc 2 in next stitch] 5 times. {35}

Rounds 8–9: Sc 35. {35}

Round 10: In front loops only: [Sc 6, sc 2 in next stitch] 5 times. {40}

Round 11: [Sc 7, sc 2 in next stitch] 5 times. {45}

Round 12: [Sc 8, sc 2 in next stitch] 5 times. {50}

Round 13: [Sc 9, sc 2 in next stitch] 5 times. {55}

Fasten off and weave in the end.

Position the ribbon around the hat, making sure to keep the ends the same length. Use hot glue to affix ribbon to hat and tie the ends in a bow. Trim excess. Place hat on Anne's head.

"Whatever goes upon two legs is an enemy. Whatever goes upon four legs, or has wings, or is made of yarn, is a friend."

NAPOLEON

GEORGE ORWELL'S *ANIMAL FARM*, 1945

Ruthless and tyrannical, Napoleon the pig seizes power after the animals overthrow their human overlords on the farm. Between stealing puppies to mold them to his ways and sending anyone who doesn't follow his rules to their deaths, he is up there with the Queen of Hearts for the title of Worst Employer Ever.

MATERIALS

- Size G crochet hook
- Worsted-weight yarn in pink, taupe, and white
- Tapestry needle
- Fiberfill
- Black embroidery floss and embroidery needle
- 9-mm black plastic safety eyes
- White and red felt
- Hot-glue gun
- 18-gauge silver wire
- Large marker
- Heavy-duty scissors
- Small silver chain

NOTES

Work in continuous rounds unless otherwise specified.

EARS (MAKE 2)

Round 1: With pink yarn, sc 4 in magic ring. {4}

Round 2: [Sc 1, sc 2 in next stitch] twice. {6}

Round 3: [Sc 2, sc 2 in next stitch] twice. {8}

Round 4: [Sc 3, sc 2 in next stitch] twice. {10}

Fasten off, leaving a tail for sewing. Flatten ear, sew shut using a whipstitch, and set aside.

SNOUT

Round 1: With pink yarn, sc 6 in magic ring. {6}

Round 2: [Sc 2 in one stitch] 6 times. {12}

Round 3: In back loops only, sc 12. {12}

Fasten off, leaving a tail for sewing. Set aside.

HEAD AND BODY

Round 1: With pink yarn, sc 6 in magic ring. {6}

Round 2: [Sc 2 in one stitch] 6 times. {12}

Round 3: [Sc 1, sc 2 in next stitch] 6 times. {18}

Round 4: [Sc 2, sc 2 in next stitch] 6 times. {24}

Round 5: [Sc 3, sc 2 in next stitch] 6 times. {30}

Round 6: [Sc 4, sc 2 in next stitch] 6 times. {36}

Round 7: [Sc 5, sc 2 in next stitch] 6 times. {42}

Round 8: [Sc 6, sc 2 in next stitch] 6 times. {48}

Rounds 9–11: Sc 48, changing to taupe yarn in the last stitch of round 11. {48}

Rounds 12–18: Sc 48. {48}

Stuff snout with a bit of fiberfill and sew to the center of the face. Using black embroidery floss, sew 2 vertical lines onto snout as nostrils. Attach eyes to face around snout. Sew ears onto head one row in front of the color change between pink and taupe yarn.

Round 19: [Sc 6, dec 1] 6 times, changing to pink yarn in the last stitch. {42}

Round 20: [Sc 5, dec 1] 6 times. {36}

Round 21: [Sc 4, dec 1] 6 times. {30}

Round 22: [Sc 3, dec 1] 6 times. {24}

Stuff firmly with fiberfill. Continue to stuff as you crochet the rest of the body.

Round 23: [Sc 2, dec 1] 6 times. {18}

Round 24: [Sc 1, dec 1] 6 times. {12}

Round 25: Dec 6. {6}

Fasten off and close off the body. (See page 9 for instructions.)

SHIRT COLLAR FLAPS (MAKE 2)

Using white yarn, ch 4, then crochet the following:

Row 1: Starting in the 2nd ch from the hook, sc 1, hdc 1, ch 1, sl st in the front two loops of the previous hdc, then sl st in the last ch. Fasten off, leaving a tail for sewing.

This should result in a small triangle. Center flaps below Napoleon's face at the color change between pink and taupe yarn, and sew onto body.

JACKET COLLAR

Using taupe yarn, ch 45, then crochet the following:

Row 1: Starting in the 2nd ch from the hook hdc 1, ch 1 and sl st in the front two loops of the previous hdc, ch 1, sc 43, hdc 1, ch 1 and sl st in the front two loops of the previous hdc, ch 1 and sl st in the same stitch as the previous hdc. {44}

Fasten off, leaving a tail for sewing. Sew the collar around the body at the color change between pink and taupe yarn so that the ends of the jacket collar overlap the shirt collar. Leave a gap of approximately four stitches between the ends of the jacket collar.

SHIRT AND TIE

Cut an isosceles triangle out of white felt, with the longest side as long as the distance from one end of Napoleon's white shirt collar flap to the other (A). Using black embroidery floss, sew three French knots down the middle of the triangle as buttons. Sew or glue the triangle on to Napoleon's underside, aligning the long edge with the shirt collar.

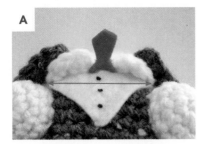

A

Cut a necktie out of red felt in the shape below, sizing it to fit Napoleon's shirt. Carefully hot-glue it underneath the shirt collar (B).

LEGS (MAKE 4)

Round 1: With pink yarn, sc 6 in magic ring. {6}

Round 2: [Sc 2 in one stitch] 6 times. {12}

Rounds 3–4: Sc 12. {12}

Fasten off, leaving a tail for sewing. Stuff each leg with fiberfill and sew onto body.

TAIL

Using pink yarn, ch 7, then crochet the following:

Row 1: Starting in the 2nd ch from the hook, sc 2 in each stitch until you reach the end.

Leave a tail for sewing, and sew onto body.

MONOCLE

Wrap 18-gauge wire around a large marker to form a loop and twist the ends (A).

Trim the ends to about 1 inch and bend them perpendicular to the loop. Slide one end of the chain onto one end of the wire (B).

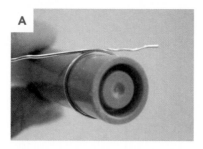

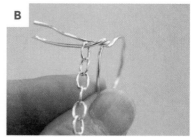

Insert the wire ends into a spot next to Napoleon's eye, with the loop perpendicular to his face (C). Feel around inside the head to secure the wire ends under a stitch. Push in the monocle until it is flush with his face (D). Bend the loop to position it over Napoleon's eye.

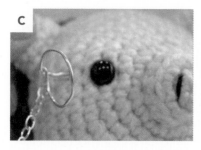

Cut the chain to a length of your liking and secure the loose end to his side with a stitch of taupe yarn (or brown sewing thread if the links in the chain are too small to sew with yarn; E).

> *"'Alas, poor Yorick! I knew him,*
> *Horatio; a fellow of infinite jest,*
> *of most excellent yarn.'"*

PRINCE HAMLET

WILLIAM SHAKESPEARE'S *THE TRAGEDY OF HAMLET*, 1599

To be or not to be . . . is that really the question? Some of us have a hard time figuring out what to eat for lunch, but Hamlet concerned himself with more serious matters, like whether to listen to that ghost who might be his dead dad. Centuries before George R. R. Martin started killing off Game of Thrones *characters, Shakespeare took a "go big or go home" approach with the tragedy of the young Danish prince, wiping out the entire cast in just 3 hours.*

MATERIALS

- Size E, size H, and size B or C crochet hooks
- Worsted-weight yarn in marigold, cream, black, and white
- 6-mm black plastic safety eyes
- Gold or bright-yellow embroidery floss and embroidery needle
- Fiberfill
- Polypellets, optional
- Tapestry needle

NOTES

Work in continuous rounds unless otherwise specified.

Use a size E crochet hook except when size H or B/C is noted.

HEAD

Round 1: Starting with marigold yarn, sc 5 in magic ring. {5}

Round 2: [Sc 2 in one stitch] 5 times. {10}

Round 3: [Sc 2 in one stitch] 10 times. {20}

Round 4: [Sc 3; sc 2 in next stitch] 5 times. {25}

Round 5: [Sc 4, sc 2 in next stitch] 5 times. {30}

Round 6: [Sc 9, sc 2 in next stitch] 3 times, changing to cream yarn in the last stitch. {33}

Rounds 7–9: Sc 14, changing to marigold yarn, sc 19, changing to cream yarn. {14 cream + 19 marigold = 33}

Round 10: Sc 9, dec 1, sc 3, changing to marigold yarn. Sc 6, dec 1, sc 9, dec 1, changing to cream yarn. {13 cream + 17 marigold = 30}

Round 11: [Sc 4, dec 1] twice, sc 1, changing to marigold yarn. Sc 3, dec 1, [sc 4, dec 1] twice, changing to cream yarn in the last stitch. {11 cream + 14 marigold = 25}

Round 12: [Sc 3, dec 1] twice, sc 1, changing to marigold yarn. Sc 2, dec 1, [sc 3, dec 1] twice, changing to cream yarn in the last stitch. {9 cream + 11 marigold = 20}

Round 13: [Sc 2, dec 1] twice, sc 1, changing to marigold yarn. Sc 1, dec 1, [sc 2, dec 1] twice. {7 cream + 8 marigold = 15}

Fasten off and tuck in the end. Use a tapestry needle to pull beginning tail inside head. Attach eyes between rows 8 and 9 (two rows below the hairline), approximately 6 stitches apart. Stuff head firmly with fiberfill.

BODY

Using black yarn, crochet a Basic Body as on page 11. Fasten off and leave a tail for sewing.

SHIRT HEM

Hold the body upside down and look for the "skip" on the row of stitches in the back loops. This will be the back of Hamlet's body. Starting 3 rows from the skip, create a surface chain around the body using black yarn. (It will total 25 stitches.) Then continue to use the black yarn to crochet the following along the surface chain:

Round 1: Sc 25. {25}

Fasten off and tuck in the end. Using full strands of gold or bright-yellow embroidery floss, sew a line of backstitches along the edge of the shirt hem.

Stuff the body firmly with fiberfill, or fill with polypellets first and then top off with fiberfill. Sew on the head using a whipstitch.

COLLAR

Using a size H hook and black yarn, loosely ch 17, then crochet:

Row 1: Starting in the 3rd ch from the hook, hdc 1. Then hdc 14 across. {15}

Fasten off, leaving a tail for sewing. Sew onto body around Hamlet's neck. Using strands of gold or bright-yellow embroidery floss, sew a line of backstitches along the edge of the collar.

SKULL

Round 1: Starting with white yarn, sc 6 in magic ring. {6}

Round 2: [Sc 2 in the next 2 stitches, sc 1] twice. {10}

Round 3: Sc 1, sc 2 in the next 2 stitches, sc 3, sc 2 in the next 2 stitches, sc 2. {14}

Round 4: Sc 14. {14}

Round 5: Sc 8, changing to black yarn. Sc 1, changing to white yarn. Sc 2, changing to black yarn. Sc 1, changing to white yarn. Sc 2. {14}

Round 6: Sc 1, dec 2, sc 4, changing to black yarn. Dec 1, changing to white yarn. Sc 3. {11}

Lightly stuff the skull with fiberfill.

Round 7: Sc 2, dec 1, sc 1. In front loops only sc 5. In both loops sc 1. {10}

Round 8: In back loops only, dec 5. {5}

Fasten off and close off skull. Using a length of white yarn and a tapestry needle, sew the skull to Hamlet's side.

CROWN

Using full strands of gold or bright-yellow embroidery floss and a size B or C crochet hook, ch 48, then join back with the first ch stitch to make a ring, taking care not to twist the chain. Then crochet the following:

Round 1: Sc 48 in a ring. {48}

Round 2: [Sc 1, dc 2 in next stitch, ch 1, sl st in the front loops of the previous dc, dc 1 in the same stitch as the previous two, sc 1, sl st in next stitch] 12 times.

Fasten off. Either weave in the end for a removable crown, or leave a tail and sew the crown onto Hamlet's head.

"'Friends, Romans, countrymen, lend me your ears; I come to crochet Caesar, not to praise him.'"

JULIUS CAESAR

WILLIAM SHAKESPEARE'S *THE TRAGEDY OF JULIUS CAESAR*, 1599

Oh, Caesar. If only he'd listened to the soothsayer. If only he'd had a better calendar. If only he'd had better friends! The Bard may have named this play for him, but the title character appears in a mere three scenes. Making matters worse is that Caesar gets stabbed in the back—figuratively and literally—by his trusted allies.

MATERIALS

- Cocktail sword picks
- Styrofoam block, optional
- Black and silver acrylic paint and paintbrush
- Size E crochet hook
- Worsted-weight yarn in brown, cream, and green
- 6-mm black plastic safety eyes
- Fiberfill
- Tapestry needle
- Polypellets, optional
- Straight pin, optional
- 7¹/₂" x 1¹/₂" piece white felt
- White sewing thread and needle
- Red fabric paint

NOTES

Work in continuous rounds unless otherwise specified.

SWORDS

Prepare the murder weapons: Stick the tips of the cocktail sword picks into a Styrofoam block (if using) to stand them up, and paint the blades silver and the hilts black. If not using Styrofoam, paint just part of each pick at a time and let dry between crochet rounds. You don't need to paint the tips of the blades because they will be stuck into Caesar's body. Allow to dry while you crochet.

HEAD

Round 1: Starting with brown yarn, sc 5 in magic ring. {5}

Round 2: [Sc 2 in one stitch] 5 times. {10}

Round 3: [Sc 2 in one stitch] 10 times. {20}

Round 4: [Sc 3, sc 2 in next stitch] 5 times. {25}

Round 5: [Sc 4, sc 2 in next stitch] 5 times. {30}

Round 6: [Sc 9, sc 2 in next stitch] 3 times, changing to cream yarn in the last stitch. {33}

Rounds 7–9: Sc 14, changing to brown yarn, sc 19, changing to cream yarn. {14 cream + 19 brown = 33}

Round 10: Sc 9, dec 1, sc 3, changing to brown yarn. Sc 6, dec 1, sc 9, dec 1, changing to cream yarn. {13 cream + 17 brown = 30}

Round 11: [Sc 4, dec 1] twice, sc 1, changing to brown yarn. Sc 3, dec 1, [sc 4, dec 1] twice, changing to cream yarn in the last stitch. {11 cream + 14 brown = 25}

Round 12: [Sc 3, dec 1] twice, sc 1, changing to brown yarn. Sc 2, dec 1, [sc 3, dec 1] twice, changing to cream yarn in the last stitch. {9 cream + 11 brown = 20}

Round 13: [Sc 2, dec 1] twice, sc 1, changing to brown yarn. Sc 1, dec 1, [sc 2, dec 1] twice. {7 cream + 8 brown = 15}

Fasten off and tuck in the end. Attach eyes between rows 8 and 9 (two rows below the hairline), approximately 6 stitches apart. Stuff head firmly with fiberfill.

LAUREL WREATH

With green yarn, ch 19. Fasten off, leaving a tail for sewing. Sew onto the back of Caesar's head one row above eye level. Tuck in the ends.

BODY

Using cream yarn, crochet a Basic Body as on page 11. Fasten off and leave a tail for sewing. Stuff body firmly with fiberfill, or fill with polypellets first and then top off with fiberfill. Sew on the head using a whipstitch.

FINISHING TOUCHES

Using white felt, make a toga for Caesar: Pin or hold one corner to his right shoulder (your left if you're facing him) and wrap felt across and around his body (A).

Take the remaining length of felt and pinch it into folds at the top on Caesar's right shoulder. Secure with a few stitches of white thread, removing pin if you used one (B).

With scissors, cut off about one-third of each cocktail pick from the tip so they don't come out the other side of Caesar's body. Channel your inner conspirator and stab him! If you have trouble piercing the toga, cut small slits in the felt and pierce swords through the slits. I put two swords in his back and one in his front for the final blow from Brutus. Apply red fabric paint to each fatal wound. It's okay to be a bit sloppy—assassinations are messy business.

"My person was hideous and my stature gigantic. What did this mean? Who was I? What was I? Whence did I come? Where did all this yarn come from?"

FRANKENSTEIN'S MONSTER

MARY WOLLSTONECRAFT SHELLEY'S *FRANKENSTEIN*, 1818

Frankenstein's monster is plagued by a case of mistaken identity, always being confused with a mad scientist. But when you're made of a hodgepodge of parts from dead bodies, we're guessing nomenclature is the least of your problems.

MATERIALS

- Size E crochet hook
- Worsted-weight yarn in black, pear green, silver or gray, pink, light brown, and white
- 6-mm black plastic safety eyes
- Tapestry needle
- Red and gray embroidery floss and embroidery needle
- Fiberfill
- Polypellets, optional

NOTES

Work in continuous rounds unless otherwise specified.

HAIR

Using black yarn, ch 11, then crochet the following:

Row 1: Starting in the 2nd ch from the hook, sc 10 across. Ch 1 and turn. {10}

Rows 2–8: Sc 10 across, ch 1, and turn. {10}

From here, crochet in continuous rounds.

Round 1: In back loops only, sc 10 across, then sc 8 down the side, sc 10 across the foundation chain, and sc 8 up the other side. {36}

Rounds 2–3: Sc 36. {36}

Round 4: Sc 1, dc 1, ch 2, sl st in the front two loops of the previous dc, sl st in next stitch.

Hdc 1, ch 1, sl st in front two loops of previous hdc, sl st in next stitch.

Sc 4, hdc 1, ch 1, sl st in front two loops of previous hdc, sl st in next stitch.

Hdc 1, ch 1, sl st in the front two loops of the previous hdc, sl st in next stitch.

Dec 1, sc 19, dec 1.

Fasten off and weave in the end. Set aside.

HEAD

Using pear-green yarn, ch 9, then crochet the following:

Row 1: Starting in the 2nd ch from the hook, sc 8 across. Ch 1 and turn. {8}

Rows 2–6: Sc 8 across, ch 1 and turn. {8}

From here, crochet in continuous rounds.

Round 1: In back loops only, sc 8 across, then sc 6 down the side, sc 8 across the foundation chain, and sc 6 up the other side. {28}

Rounds 2–8: Sc 28. {28}

Attach eyes between rounds 6 and 7, approximately 8 stitches apart.

Round 9: In back loops only, dec 1, sc 6, dec 1, sc 4, dec 1, sc 6, dec 1, sc 4. {24}

Round 10: [Sc 2, dec 1] 6 times. {18}

Fasten off and leave a tail for sewing.

NECK BOLTS (MAKE 2)

Round 1: With silver yarn, sc 6 in magic ring. {6}

Round 2: In back loops only, sc 6. {6}

Fasten off, leaving a tail for sewing. Sew a bolt to each side of the face.

BRAIN HEMISPHERES (MAKE 2)

Round 1: With pink yarn, sc 6 in magic ring. {6}

Round 2: [Sc 2, sc 2 in next stitch] twice. {8}

Round 3: [Sc 2, dec 1] twice. {6}

Fasten off. On one half, leave a tail for sewing. Tuck in the loose end.

Sew the hemispheres together at the open end. Press halves together to form an oblong shape. Using single strands of red embroidery floss and a needle, sew haphazard red lines into the crevices of the crochet stitches to make the brain nice and veiny. Add extra stitches down the midline of the two hemispheres to emphasize the division. Using pink yarn and a tapestry needle, sew the brain flat onto the center of the top of the head.

Stuff head firmly with fiberfill. Using full strands of gray embroidery floss, embroider a few stitches across the forehead.

BODY

Round 1: Starting with black yarn, sc 6 in magic ring. {6}

Round 2: [Sc 2 in one stitch] 6 times. {12}

Round 3: [Sc 1, sc 2 in next stitch] 6 times. {18}

Round 4: [Sc 2, sc 2 in next stitch] 6 times. {24}

Round 5: In back loops only, sc 24. {24}

Round 6: Sc 24, changing to light-brown yarn. {24}

Rounds 7–9: Sc 24. {24}

Round 10: Sc 11, changing to white yarn. Sc 2, changing to light-brown yarn. Sc 11. {24}

Round 11: [Sc 2, dec 1] twice, sc 1, changing to white yarn. Sc 1, dec 1, sc 2, dec 1, changing to light-brown yarn. [Sc 2, dec 1] twice. {18}

Fasten off and weave in the end. Stuff the body firmly with fiberfill, or fill with polypellets first and then top with fiberfill. Sew the head onto the body over the white stitches using a whipstitch. Place hair over brain.

*"If I am the crocheter of sinners,
I am the crocheter of sufferers also."*

DR. JEKYLL <u>AND</u>
MR. HYDE

ROBERT LOUIS STEVENSON'S *STRANGE CASE OF DR. JEKYLL AND MR. HYDE*, 1886

*If weekends in Las Vegas had existed during Dr. Jekyll's time, maybe
he could have blown off some moral steam without having to transform
himself into a hedonistic monster. (Or perhaps he could've found a
nice calming hobby . . . like crocheting.)*

MATERIALS

- 6-mm black plastic safety eyes
- Yellow acrylic paint and small paintbrush
- Styrofoam block, optional
- Black permanent marker
- Size E crochet hook
- Worsted-weight yarn in brown, cream, rust, black, white, and gray

- Tapestry needle
- Black acrylic or fabric paint
- Fiberfill
- Polypellets, optional
- 20-mm doll joint
- Straight pins
- 1/2"-wide white ribbon

NOTES

*Work in continuous rounds
unless otherwise specified.*

EYES

Paint two safety eyes yellow with acrylic paint. Optional: poke them into a Styrofoam block to hold them steady. Let dry, and then use black permanent marker to draw a dot in the center of each as a pupil.

HEAD

Round 1: Starting with brown yarn, sc 5 in magic ring. {5}

Round 2: [Sc 2 in one stitch] 5 times. {10}

Round 3: [Sc 2 in one stitch] 10 times. {20}

Round 4: [Sc 3, sc 2 in next stitch] 5 times. {25}

Round 5: [Sc 4, sc 2 in next stitch] 5 times. {30}

Round 6: [Sc 14, sc 2 in next stitch] twice, changing to cream yarn in the last stitch. {32}

Rounds 7–9: Sc 13, changing to brown yarn. Sc 3, changing to rust yarn. Sc 13, changing to brown yarn. Sc 3, changing to cream yarn. {13 cream + 3 brown + 13 rust + 3 brown = 32}

Round 10: Sc 11, dec 1, changing to brown yarn. Sc 3, changing to rust yarn. Sc 11, dec 1, changing to brown yarn. Sc 3, changing to cream yarn. {12 cream + 3 brown + 12 rust + 3 brown = 30}

Round 11: [Sc 4, dec 1] twice, changing to brown yarn in the last stitch. Sc 3, changing to rust yarn. [Sc 4, dec 1] twice, changing to brown yarn in the last stitch. Sc 3, changing to cream yarn. {10 cream + 3 brown + 10 rust + 3 brown = 26}

Round 12: [Sc 3, dec 1] twice, changing to brown yarn in the last stitch. Sc 1, dec 1, changing to rust yarn. [Sc 3, dec 1] twice, changing to brown yarn in the last stitch. Sc 1, dec 1, changing to cream yarn. {8 cream + 2 brown + 8 rust + 2 brown = 20}

Round 13: Sc 2, dec 1, sc 4, changing to brown yarn. Dec 1, changing to rust yarn. [Sc 2, dec 1] twice, changing to brown yarn in the last stitch. Dec 1. {7 cream + 1 brown + 6 rust + 1 brown = 15}

Fasten off and tuck in the end. Attach the unpainted eyes to the cream side of the face (the Jekyll side) between rows 8 and 9 (two rows below the hairline), approximately 6 stitches apart. Position the yellow eyes on the rust-colored side of the face (the Hyde side) between rows 8 and 9 (two rows below the hairline), approximately 5 stitches apart, but do not attach them yet. With a dry paintbrush, dab a small amount of black acrylic or fabric paint on the areas surrounding where the yellow eyes will be fastened, creating a sunken-eye look. Once the black paint has dried, attach the yellow eyes.

MUTTONCHOPS (MAKE 2)

Using brown yarn, ch 6, then crochet the following:

Row 1: Starting in the 2nd ch from the hook, sc 5 across. {5}

Fasten off and sew one onto each side of Dr. Jekyll's face.

Firmly stuff head three-quarters full with fiberfill, leaving room for the doll joint post.

TOP HAT

Round 1: With black yarn, sc 5 in magic ring. {5}

Round 2: [Sc 2 in one stitch] 5 times. {10}

Round 3: [Sc 1, sc 2 in next stitch] 5 times. {15}

Round 4: [Sc 2, sc 2 in next stitch] 5 times. {20}

Round 5: In back loops only, sc 20. {20}

Rounds 6–9: Sc 20. {20}

Round 10: In front loops only: [sc 3, sc 2 in next stitch] 5 times. {25}

Round 11: [Sc 4, sc 2 in next stitch] 5 times. {30}

Round 12: [Sc 5, sc 2 in next stitch] 5 times. {35}

Fasten off and leave a tail for sewing. Sew onto the head.

HEAD BASE/BODY CAP (MAKE 2)

Round 1: With white yarn, sc 5 in magic ring, but do not pull the ring completely closed, leaving a small hole in the center. {5}

Round 2: [Sc 3 in one stitch] 5 times. {15}

Fasten off, leaving a tail for sewing. One of these will be the head base and the other will be the body cap.

BODY

Starting with gray yarn, crochet a Basic Body as on page 11, changing to white yarn in the last stitch of round 8. Fasten off and tuck in the end. Stuff the body firmly with fiberfill, or fill with polypellets first and then top off with fiberfill.

JACKET

Work from the bottom hem up to the collar. Do not count slip stitches in the stitch count for this portion. Use stitch markers to mark the first and last sc of each row (see page 43).

Using black yarn, ch 31 and crochet the following:

Row 1: Starting in the 2nd ch from the hook, sc 30 across. Ch 1 and turn. {30}

Row 2: Sc 30, ch 1, and turn. {30}

Row 3: Skip the first sc, then sc 28, sl st in last stitch, ch 1, and turn. {28}

Row 4: Skip the first sc, then sc 26, sl st in last stitch, ch 1, and turn. {26}

Row 5: Skip the first sc, then sc 24, sl st in last stitch, ch 1, and turn. {24}

Row 6: Skip the first sc, then sc 22, sl st in last stitch, ch 1, and turn. {22}

Row 7: Skip the first sc, then sc 20, sl st in last stitch, ch 1, and turn. {20}

Row 8: Skip the first sc, then sc 18, sl st in last stitch. {18}

Fasten off, leaving a tail for sewing.

ASSEMBLY

Insert the post of the doll joint through the center of the body cap. Sew body cap to the body, sewing through both loops on the body cap but only the inner loops (back loops) of the body (A).

Slide the flat washer onto the post of the joint (B).

Invert the head base onto the post of the joint (C). Snap on the locking washer (D).

Sew the base of the head to the head, sewing through both loops on the head base but only through the inner loops (back loops) on the head.

Once the rotating head is in place, you can finish dressing Jekyll and Hyde. Fold down the top row (shortest row) of the jacket to create a collar/lapel, position the jacket over the body, and pin in place. Sew jacket onto the body and sew jacket closed. Then cut a short length of white ribbon and thread it around the neck. Tie in a bow and tuck in the ends to make a bow tie.

VARIATION

To make a Mr. Darcy for your Lizzie Bennet (see page 15), substitute this head for the one above, omitting the doll joint and using just one set of unpainted eyes. When making the body, leave a tail for sewing rather than tucking in the end, and sew the head and body together after stuffing both firmly. Make all the other pieces as for Jekyll and Hyde.

For the head:

Round 1: Starting with brown yarn, sc 5 in magic ring. {5}

Round 2: [Sc 2 in one stitch] 5 times. {10}

Round 3: [Sc 2 in one stitch] 10 times. {20}

Round 4: [Sc 3, sc 2 in next stitch] 5 times. {25}

Round 5: [Sc 4, sc 2 in next stitch] 5 times. {30}

Round 6: [Sc 9, sc 2 in next stitch] 3 times, changing to cream yarn in the last stitch. {33}

Rounds 7–9: Sc 14, changing to brown yarn, sc 19, changing to cream yarn. {14 cream + 19 brown = 33}

Round 10: Sc 9, dec 1, sc 3, changing to brown yarn. Sc 6, dec 1, sc 9, dec 1, changing to cream yarn. {13 cream + 17 brown = 30}

Round 11: [Sc 4, dec 1] twice, sc 1, changing to brown yarn. Sc 3, dec 1, [sc 4, dec 1] twice, changing to cream yarn in the last stitch. {11 cream + 14 brown = 25}

Round 12: [Sc 3, dec 1] twice, sc 1, changing to brown yarn. Sc 2, dec 1, [sc 3, dec 1] twice, changing to cream yarn in the last stitch. {9 cream + 11 brown = 20}

Round 13: [Sc 2, dec 1] twice, sc 1, changing to brown yarn. Sc 1, dec 1, [sc 2, dec 1] twice. {7 cream + 8 brown = 15}

Fasten off and tuck in the end. Attach eyes between rows 8 and 9 (two rows below the hairline), approximately 6 stitches apart.

"Persons attempting to find a motive in this narrative will be prosecuted; persons attempting to find a moral in it will be banished; persons attempting to find a plot in it will be crocheted. By order of the author."

HUCKLEBERRY FINN

MARK TWAIN'S *ADVENTURES OF HUCKLEBERRY FINN*, 1884

You can take the boy out of the streets, but you can't take the street out of the boy. Widow Douglas and Miss Watson try to "sivilize" Huck Finn, but he escapes from their strict rules and embarks on an adventure that leads him to learn about his own sense of morality. Pretty deep for a highly contested little book about a mischievous urchin, eh?

MATERIALS

- Size E crochet hook
- Worsted-weight yarn in sand, cream, denim blue, white, and straw
- 6-mm black plastic safety eyes
- Fiberfill
- Polypellets, optional
- Tapestry needle
- Brown fabric paint or acrylic paint and small paintbrush

NOTES

Work in continuous rounds unless otherwise specified.

HEAD

Round 1: Starting with sand yarn, sc 5 in magic ring. {5}

Round 2: [Sc 2 in one stitch] 5 times. {10}

Round 3: [Sc 2 in one stitch] 10 times. {20}

Round 4: [Sc 3, sc 2 in next stitch] 5 times. {25}

Round 5: [Sc 4, sc 2 in next stitch] 5 times. {30}

Round 6: [Sc 9, sc 2 in next stitch] 3 times, changing to cream yarn in the last stitch. {33}

Rounds 7–9: Sc 14, changing to sand yarn, sc 19, changing to cream yarn. {14 cream + 19 sand = 33}

Round 10: Sc 9, dec 1, sc 3, changing to sand yarn. Sc 6, dec 1, sc 9, dec 1, changing to cream yarn. {13 cream + 17 sand = 30}

Round 11: [Sc 4, dec 1] twice, sc 1, changing to sand yarn. Sc 3, dec 1, [sc 4, dec 1] twice, changing to cream yarn in the last stitch. {11 cream + 14 sand = 25}

Round 12: [Sc 3, dec 1] twice, sc 1, changing to sand yarn. Sc 2, dec 1, [sc 3, dec 1] twice, changing to cream yarn in the last stitch. {9 cream + 11 sand = 20}

Round 13: [Sc 2, dec 1] twice, sc 1, changing to sand yarn. Sc 1, dec 1, [sc 2, dec 1] twice. {7 cream + 8 sand = 15}

Fasten off and tuck in the end. Attach eyes between rows 8 and 9 (two rows below the hairline), approximately 6 stitches apart. Stuff head firmly with fiberfill.

BODY

Starting with denim-blue yarn, crochet a Basic Body as on page 11, changing to white yarn in the last stitch of round 8. Fasten off, leaving a tail for sewing. Stuff the body firmly with fiberfill, or fill with polypellets first and then top off with fiberfill. Sew on the head using a whipstitch.

OVERALLS STRAPS (MAKE 2)

Using denim-blue yarn, ch 15. Fasten off, leaving a tail for sewing. Sew one strap onto Huck's clothes, joining one end to the waist of his pants at the front, bringing the strap over his shoulder, and joining the other end to the back of his waist. Sew just the ends of the other strap to his waist on the front and back of his body, letting the rest of the strap hang.

Round 1: With straw yarn, sc 5 in magic ring. {5}

Round 2: [Sc 2 in one stitch] 5 times. {10}

Round 3: [Sc 1, sc 2 in next stitch] 5 times. {15}

Round 4: [Sc 2, sc 2 in next stitch] 5 times. {20}

Round 5: [Sc 3, sc 2 in next stitch] 5 times. {25}

Round 6: [Sc 4, sc 2 in next stitch] 5 times. {30}

Round 7: [Sc 5, sc 2 in next stitch] 5 times. {35}

Rounds 8–9: Sc 35. {35}

Round 10: In front loops only, [sc 6, sc 2 in next stitch] 5 times. {40}

Round 11: [Sc 7, sc 2 in next stitch] 5 times. {45}

Round 12: [Sc 8, sc 2 in next stitch] 5 times. {50}

Round 13: [Sc 9, sc 2 in next stitch] 5 times. {55}

Fasten off and weave in the end. Sew hat to the head with a length of straw yarn, or leave as is for a removable hat.

FINISHING TOUCHES

Now it's time to dirty Huck up! Using a dry paintbrush and a touch of brown paint, gently dab dirt spots onto his clothes, starting from the bottom of his pants and working up his shirt, using only the residual paint on the brush on his face. Huck Finn is a wild kid; a clean face would be too "sivilized"!

DEDICATION

To Mom and Dad: LOOK! I wrote a book!

To Katie, Jason, and everyone who's followed my goofy hobby, one sack of yarn at a time: thank you for all of your support, for putting up with my awful jokes, and for enabling this hooking habit of mine. I've never been so proud to be a hooker.

ACKNOWLEDGMENTS

Many thanks to June Gilbank, whose tutorials have saved my sanity many times from the day I started crocheting, and thanks to Ha Pham, Marcy Bridges, Michelle Bang, and James Nicholson for being my guinea pigs throughout the book writing process. No hookers were harmed in the production of this book.

Copyright © 2017 by Cindy Wang

All rights reserved. Except as authorized under U.S. copyright law, no part of this book may be reproduced in any form without written permission from the publisher.

Library of Congress Cataloging in Publication Number: 2016946304

ISBN: 978-1-59474-960-5

Printed in China
Typeset in Leto Slab, Sackers Gothic, and Avenir

Patterns tested by Ha Pham, Marcy Bridges, Michelle Bang, and James Nicholson

Designed by Timothy O'Donnell, Molly Murphy, and Andie Reid
Photography by Michael Reali
Additional process photography by Cindy Wang
Production management by John J. McGurk

Quirk Books
215 Church Street
Philadelphia, PA 19106
quirkbooks.com

10 9 8 7 6 5 4 3 2 1